GLIMPSES
of Heaven

A true account of spiritual journeys

GLIMPSES
of Heaven

A true account of spiritual journeys

RICHARD S. SMITH

DocUmeant *Publishing*
244 5th Avenue
Suite G-200
NY, NY 10001
646-233-4366
www.DocUmeantPublishing.com

Published by
DocUmeant Publishing
244 5th Avenue, Suite G-200
NY, NY 10001

Phone: 646-233-4366

Glimpses *of Heaven*

Cover art "Stairway to Heaven" by Jim Warren used with permission

Illustrations by Ginger Marks, DocUmeantDesigns.com

Library of Congress Control Number: 2017949900

ISBN: 978-1-9378-0184-7

Contents

Foreword

I was first approached by Richard in 2015 to review his book, *A Glimpses of Heaven*. Having edited scores of books in every Christian genre, I was intrigued by the uniqueness of his material. Heaven is the eternal home for those of us who have placed our faith for salvation in the finished work of Jesus Christ when He paid the price for our sins at Calvary.

Someone once said Christians are truly a peculiar people. We believe a story we can't prove, we love a person we've never met, and we're homesick for a place we've never been to. There is a great deal of truth in this statement, for these are the things that motivate all those who are truly born again. There is a wonderful hymn titled *"My Savior First of All,"* that talks about how of all the things we long to see in heaven, the first and greatest is Jesus, the one who died for us.

In the past several years there has been a renewed emphasis on heaven among Christians and even the lost who are currently on the outside looking in. Movies such as *God's Not Dead* deal with the subject by having an atheist who had spent his life mocking God realizing he wants to go to heaven as he is dying after being hit by a car. A well-known book that became a best-seller is "*Heaven is for Real: A Little Boy's Astounding Story of His Trip to Heaven and Back.*"

My purpose is not to become involved in the debate over whether the experiences recounted by Richard Smith are real or not. Rather, I am pointing out that deep in the human heart is a longing for an afterlife and a place called heaven, regardless of what one may call it. The late Carl Sagan said in an interview towards the end of his life that he wished there was evidence for him to believe in an afterlife. Jackie Gleason said in an interview just days before he died that he wished there was some way he could know for sure he would go to Heaven.

In this book, Richard relates his experiences during his own trips to heaven to meet Jesus and other people from the Bible and history. He is an ordained minister and comes from a family of preachers. As such, he is well-acquainted with what the Bible has to say on these and other subjects.

Among the many things you will read in this book, you will see Richard's as well as God's burden for the lost who are on their way to hell. You will also see Jesus' disgust towards those who only pretend to play church, like those He referred to in 3 Revelation who attended the church at Laodicea.

There may be many who are skeptical of the accounts presented in this book. I would simply ask you to keep an open mind as you read, and if nothing else, come away with the idea that heaven is a real place and it is perfect where there is no pain or sorrow. It is a place where people will forever love the one who died for them. I also hope and pray you will get a burden for souls, doing your part to help them go to this wonderful place rather than spend an eternity in the Lake of Fire reserved for the Devil and his angels.

Pastor Jack Minor

Acknowledgments

I would like to express my heartfelt gratitude and love for my lovely wife Josephine Smith for being a wonderful help mate and encouraging me all these years. I would also like to thank Jack Minor, who as a pastor, shares a love for Jesus as well as having a burden for the lost.

I would also like to thank Ginger Marks of DocUmeant Publishing, for her brilliant assistance and advice. Her suggestion to use illustrations rather than photos in this book, and then generously giving of her time and talents to draw them, both surprised and delighted me.

As she was busily formatting and drawing she used her digital design talents to create the chapter decoration, which she informs me are called mandalas and are based on the ancient stained- glass windows we are so accustomed to seeing in our churches and synagogues. Her cross embellishments are just the perfect touch to pull it all together and I trust you will appreciate all her hard work as much as I do.

Introduction

Born two and a half months premature and weighting two pounds three ounces, I was the size of my mother's hand. They hurried me into an incubator with round the clock monitoring. The doctors and nurses didn't think I was going to make it. My loving mother wanted to hold me one last time to say good-bye. A local priest was called to my bedside where my mother held me tight. He gave me the last rites. To everybody's astonishment I made it past the first couple of days. The Lord had a definite plan for my life.

I was raised in a Christian home, born again at the age of five. My grandfather was a minister and I would spend my summers at their place. I would tend the garden and prepare the vegetables for supper. I would also attend every service at the church which was only half a block away from their house.

From my very young years until now, I have always striven to get closer to the Lord in my daily life as most born again Christians do. But, in 2009 the Lord Jesus Christ started to visit my house. Sometimes He would just walk through one of the walls, other times He would show up at the foot of my bed to have a conversation with me.

It has progressed over the years and now I don't need the Lord to take me by the hand in order to visit Heaven.

There are wonders beyond your wildest imagination, where physics don't apply like on Earth. Take angels for instance. They come and go at will, some fly with wings and some don't have wings but still fly. Heaven is much more than a gated city—it goes far beyond that. Since the Lord is always creating new things there is always something different to see.

Will you see your loved ones again after they have passed on? Of course you will. They will be waiting for you. Meeting some of the disciples is always exciting. But, what's most exciting is meeting the Lord, talking to him face to face, and walking hand in hand with him. Walking down streets of gold which is not like the gold we are used to seeing here.

After all the wonders I have experienced, how could I possibly keep them to myself? Jesus was moved with compassion to heal people, likewise I am moved with compassion to share with you my excitement and experiences.

There is so much more to heaven than I could possibly tell you. That's why it's called *Glimpses of Heaven*.

GLIMPSES
of Heaven

A Personal Message from Jesus Himself

My message is still the same as it was over two thousand years ago, when I died on the cross. Two people were put to death with me. They were living for themselves, getting what they could out of life, doing whatever they pleased.

One person that day accepted me as their Lord and Savior. The other person was content with the way he had been living—no regrets.

It is the same today. Are you living for yourself getting all you can before your body expires? Or have you committed to following me and my righteousness? The choice is yours. Remember the two men that died that day? I died for all mankind. My blood washes away all sin, I'm waiting with open arms for you to come home—after all it's where you came from in the first place.

Hot Air Balloon

I ask the Lord when would be the next time I could come see him, and He answered, "Today!" With this visit being imminent, I now have to talk to some people I know about hell and let them know that the Lord still occasionally visits those who go there after they die. They asked me why I said this to them. I explained the reason was because God still loves those in hell. He created them and wished that they had chosen life rather than death. Also people have asked me if I still visit the Lord. My answer is yes, every week.

The Lord appears to be getting impatient and asks, "So, are you coming, my son?"

"Yes Lord," I respond.

I am now on the outskirts of Heaven, looking at the so-called pearly gates. They are so named because the Bible records that each one is fashioned from a single pearl. However to me, they do not appear to be white like a pearl, rather they seem to be more like glass. The gates are made up of all different colors, and make a variety of sounds.

I run my hands up and down each of the different gate rungs, and of course, the Lord is watching me as I do all of this. He has a twinkle in his eye, so I know he's up to something. I look at him and ask, "What? What do you have for me Lord?"

"Just wait and see."

Suddenly a big black cat walks up to me. "Wow!" I exclaim. At first it looks like Ming-Ming, a black cat that I used to have, but looking closer I realize that it's another cat that looks as big as Ming-Ming did.

"This is Freddy, my son," the Lord says smiling.

"But what is your surprise Lord?"

"Come with me."

We walk through the front gates and past the duck pond, that's when I see the big hot air balloon.

"Lord," I exclaim in utter excitement, "Are we going up in that?"

He laughs and says, "Yes we are!" Oh boy, I make a mad dash for the balloon and jump into the basket. Once inside I call out, "All aboard!" The next thing I know the Lord jumps in beside me.

As I look around it dawns on me that I didn't see any propane cylinders to fuel the burners to lift the balloon. In spite of this I observe that the balloon is being filled even as I speak.

"Where are we going, Lord?"

"Oh, just around my son. I thought we would go to the other side of Heaven, since you have seen so little of it; only the area on this side."

We begin to rise despite not having the cylinders that would be needed if we were on Earth. Faster and faster we rise, and then we begin to move in a southerly direction. As we fly along our way I can see people waving to us and hear them say, "Look, it's the Lord with Richard the part-timer." I hear this over and over, but it's okay, I don't mind. I am now able to see some long buildings that are made up of light brown stone.

However, what is interesting is that in the midst of all of this I do not see much glass.

"Lord, what's that building for," I asked. Pointing to one He replies, "People live there like they would in an apartment. Many people think when you get to Heaven you're just going to live in a big huge house somewhere, but that is not necessarily so. Some people just want to live in these types of buildings; others are told to."

"Why"?

"Because of the many works they neglected to do while they were on Earth."

"You mean . . ."

"Yes," He says. "A lot of people are just going to squeeze into my kingdom. Most of these people will find themselves living in these types of buildings. Also, they can't see my Father. Many of them are just content to be living anywhere in Heaven. These are the facts, my son."

"If you love me you will want to do my will and there won't be any problem when you get to Heaven."

I see a river flowing northwest of us. It looks quite deep in some places. The Lord says, "That's the river you swam in before, it's just not as wide at this point."

The previous conversation we had about the apartment building began replaying itself in my mind. Knowing this, the Lord said to me, "The tears that I wipe away are the tears of

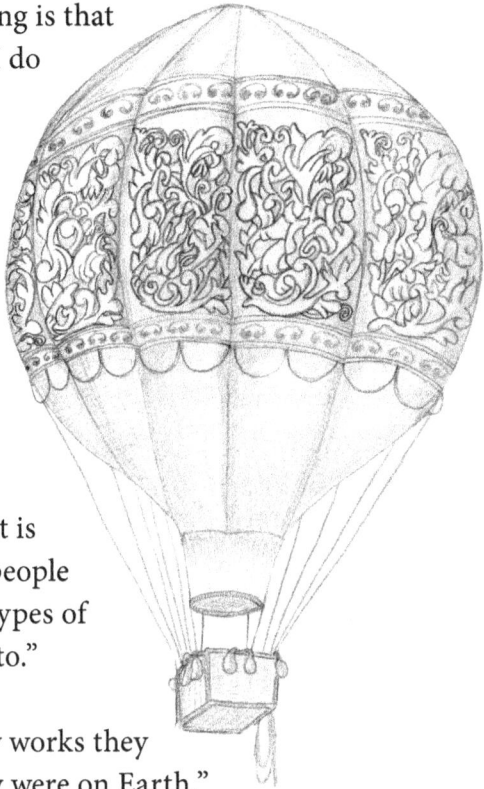

not doing what I have required, thus they are the result of not receiving a reward."

"Lord, I grew up thinking there will be big homes for every one when they get here."

He looked at me with eyes of compassion and said. "Yes my son, most people think that is so. What if I asked them to constantly do things they continued to refuse, saying 'No . . . no . . . no'? What should I do with them? Do I put them in a house like those who have obeyed and loved me while on earth? How then should I reward the ones who have done my will for years?"

"Lord," I exclaimed. "I get your point. I thought the rewards were just a crown with diamonds and precious stones."

He laughed, "No, that's just part of it."

After saying this He turns the balloon around and we started to head for home. As we touched down He said, "I hoped you learned a lot today my son."

"Oh yes." We hugged and said goodbye, and I know my time is up.

Tree House

"Well here I am again Lord, tugging at your hemline; wanting to get closer. You said it would be okay to come tonight."

The Lord responds, "I'm here now."

He arrives just like that. He has on a pair of light blue dress pants with a white silk shirt and black shoes. "Lord, you look wonderful, as always."

"Why, thank you for saying so, my son?" I just nod my head in response. "Would you like to go now?"

"No, can we just sit and chat?"

"Of course we can, what would you like to talk about, my son?"

"Oh Lord, I don't know."

The thought of asking him how old He was just popped into my head.

"I know you're quite old but you look like you're only 32 or 33."

"Well, I only aged when I was on Earth, but now you are seeing me for who I am."

"Yes Lord, I understand, kind of. Who makes up your wardrobe?"

"My son," He said, laughing. "No one does. All you have to do is think of a thing and it appears, just like all your milk shakes and food. It's the same with clothes. One only has to think about it and it's there."

The Lord announces, "I have a surprise for you!" I get excited, knowing his surprises are always simply astounding. "Shall we go now my son?"

"Yes."

In the blink of an eye we are outside the gates of heaven in one of the many fields surrounding the Holy City. We come to a forest-like setting; the Lord is ahead of me. Catching up, I grab hold of his sleeve as we start moving into the forest. My nose becomes inundated by an incredible variety of smells. There are so many it is difficult to sort them all out.

Up ahead I see a massive tree house that rivals anything produced by Hollywood. The exterior walls are a light gray, surrounding the massive trunk which stands like a great pillar in the home's center. The structure sits up in the tree nearly 40 feet above the ground, and has a porch wrapping all around before connecting to a smaller structure in a nearby tree with a similar configuration. The main section is reached by a ladder made of wood and rope. I look at the Lord and He gestures with his hand, "Go ahead."

Climbing up the ladder, when I get to the top I push up on part of the floor that opens up to allow me access to the main structure. The Lord is right behind me. Looking around, I notice in the middle of the living room is a couch with two chairs on each side. I walk over to the kitchen; it doesn't have a refrigerator or stove, just cupboards with dishes, glasses, and gold utensils. The marble sink with matching countertop is graced with a gleaming, golden faucet.

Adjacent to the kitchen is a bathroom. There is no commode or a place to put the toilet paper. It does have a fancy sink made up of the finest marble.

Off to one side is a tub. The faucets are separate to match the sink ones. Just above the tub are a set of sliding windows which overlook the forest.

We then proceed to a set of sliding windows opposite a couch, in the living room that leads to the balcony. I can see for miles and miles. The balcony has an extra table and chairs which can be used for eating as well.

Now, moving to the bedroom I spy a gigantic bed, larger than a king sized one. The bed sheet is made of a golden material with matching red pillows and has a dresser on either side.

I turn to the Lord saying, "Thank you, it's everything I ever dreamed of!"

Following the completion of the tour, we return to the living room where I plop on the couch beside the Lord. Laying my head on his breast I can feel his heart beating as his chest rises and falls. As my mind begins to drift off into nothingness once again I'm interrupted by the Lord saying, "My son, it's time for you to be going."

I look up into his loving eyes and ask, "Can I stay just five more minutes?"

He smiles down at me and in a gentle voice responds, "Sure."

The five minutes fly by so fast that before I know it they have passed, so we get up and hug and instantly I find myself back in my home on Earth.

Roller Skating

I really had to crucify my flesh tonight. There was a show on television I had been yearning to see, but earlier in the day the Lord had told me that He would visit me later this afternoon. It is now approaching Sunday evening, and despite what my flesh may desire to do, the Lord always wins. My experiences are always fulfilling in heaven and much better than anything on the "boob tube." I hear the Lord saying, "Come my son. I have been waiting for you."

I'm sorry Lord, the world kind of got in my way this afternoon. But, now that all seems like a distant memory as I am once again in his presence. We arrive approximately three blocks outside of the pearly gates. "Lord," I ask, "can we go roller skating?"

"Sure," He responds.

In an instant I have a pair of pure white leather skates on and the Lord is wearing a black leather pair.

The Lord announces, "I want to show you some new things you haven't experienced before." We turn around and start down one of the side streets at a brisk pace. While my sense of direction is poor at best, I think we are going south. I shout out to the Lord because at this point He is behind me.

"Where to?"

He replies, "Straight up ahead," as we coast up to one of the buildings. We are in what you would call a rural neighborhood. The building has an unusual layout for a roller skating rink. It seems more like a factory! Looking down at our feet, we have shoes on that weren't there just a second ago!

Walking up the steps, we open the doors and to my amazement I see children playing on all manner of playground equipment including swings, monkey bars, and some kind of structure that looks like plastic tubes they climb in and out of. Turning to the Lord I comment, "I thought children only liked playing outside."

"Well, they do, but indoors is where they have the most fun because they have everything in one place."

I look up at what appears to be a cart on a wire with a child in it, going from one end of the room to the other. The cart travels up a flight of stairs to a platform where several children are waiting in line. When the cart arrives its child cargo gets out and another one jumps in. In the cart is a pair of handles which seems to be what makes it go.

"That sure looks like a lot of fun." The Lord just laughs. Then, forgetting that my every desire comes to pass, no sooner had the words left my mouth than I find myself in my own cart. I begin slowly at first in order to get the feel of it. Wow, what a rush. Once I arrive at the other end I step out onto the platform and take the steps the rest of the way down.

"I thought you would like it my son."

"How come you never brought me here before?"

"It was not yet time."

"Oh, okay" was my only response. He put his hand on my shoulder saying, "You have to go now my son."

"Okay Lord," I sadly reply.

Merry-Go-Round

The Lord has been waiting patiently for me to just sit down and spend time with him. I'm discovering that this old world wants to siphon more and more time out of a person. The Lord says to me "Are you ready my son?"

I reply, "Yes Lord," and once again I am here in heaven. I would really like to stay in heaven forever, but I don't even bother asking because I already know his answer.

That's probably the reason he's smiling right now; He has read my mind, again. "Well, my son," He says, dressed all in white today. We are standing at the front gates when He goes on to say, "So my son, where would you like to go today?"

I have to rub my ears a little. It sounds like He just asked me where I would like to go. He says, "Yes, you heard me correctly!" laughing at the same time.

I sit down on the grass beside the main road leading in and out of heaven. Sipping a chocolate milkshake helps me think.

"I really don't know Lord."

"Well," He says, "let's go for a little walk." So, we start walking west from the front gates, but still inside them. I happen to see a merry-go-round in the distance. Wow, there are so many kids. "Lord," I yell with excitement. "Can I go?"

"Sure," He says. I run up to it stunned at how beautiful the ride looks. The first thing that catches my eye is the big gold pole in the middle of each horse. It has a spiral pattern from top to bottom and appears to be made of pure gold.

The horses are all different colors and, unlike those back on Earth, they are not made of plastic. They have short hair and real leather saddles. I jump up on a white horse. Even though the merry-go-round is not going very fast it's still thrilling. I spy some other adults here as well.

Speaking of the adults the Lord says to me, "It is very hard for many of them to remember how to play like children again, but I notice you have no problem."

"Yeah Lord," I quip as we start walking away from the Merry-Go-Round. Instantly, we are walking up a grassy hill and keep on until we are at the top. It's pretty high. I run down the other side arms and legs flying in every direction, but the Lord takes his time coming down. I see a group of teeter totters. *Some of you may know what I'm talking about while others may not.* I run over to them excitedly; the Lord follows. They are pink, red, orange, and bright yellow. I climb onto the pink one. The handles are made of gold. I try my best to bump the Lord's behind, but

I just can't do it. We go on from there, passing a fairly large stream. The water looks enticing, so I jump in without hesitation. The Lord starts laughing. I try to splash him, but He always moves just in time.

When I get out of the water, I'm completely dry. "Well my son, it's almost time for you to go again." I ask him why and He says, "My son, you can come any time you like you know. You don't have to ask, just think of me and you'll be here!"

"Yeah Lord, it's just that I forget what you're telling me. I'll have to make a point of remembering."

"That's okay. Now really, you must return. I have kingdom business to take care of." I give him a hug.

Childlike Ways

Remembering when I would run through fields of flowers
without a care in the world,
the sun glistening on my skin,
while the wind whispered through my hair.
I knew within myself that someday I would grow up.
That little boy someday would be lost.

Childlike innocence that I held so closely to my chest,
the world would say "Grow up little one,
you're not a child anymore."

Grown-ups; they're all the same.
They don't laugh and play,
perhaps they have forgotten
the childlike ways.

My mother gently combing through my hair,
her voice singing a melody of some sort.
Tears would well up as I listened to her singing ever so softly,
reminiscing of those happy days gone by.

Glimpses of Heaven

Sometimes those childhood memories flood my mind,
ever so vividly they have stood the test of time.
People don't really understand what it is like
to let the little child come from the inside out.

Now I have to say, I'm not as old as I look,
but, I'm still holding onto my childlike ways.

Marriage Preparations

It's now 10:30 at night and standing beside me in his white robe is the Lord of the universe. He is wearing his usual sandals. I blurt out sleepily, "I'm ready."

We travel upward and go through the roof at the same time. Now we are in heaven. We arrive among a grove of trees. Each tree bears a different kind of fruit. There are pear, orange, and apple trees among them. Wow.

The Lord hands me a pear. "You know I don't like pears, no way, no how!" But, I took it any way. It is super sweet, like it's made of pure sugar.

We walk over to a peach tree. I take one bite and it is just as sweet as the pear, but it still tastes like a peach. I see people dancing, but I don't hear any music! The Lord notices my puzzlement and says, "They're making the melody in their hearts. I know if you were to start dancing on Earth without any music playing people would think you were nuts!" As we begin walking away some children surround us asking to play a game called Hop-Scotch with them.

Later, I notice some of the angels are carrying packages wrapped with expensive paper and ribbons. One of the angels approaches the Lord and stands there as if awaiting instructions. The Lord asks him, "Is she ready?"

To which the angel replies, "Yes, Lord."

He waves his hand and commands, "Go." The package the angel is holding is pink with a lighter color bow on top.

The Lord looks at me and smiles. "It's a pair of dancing shoes for a twelve-year-old girl. She's been asking me for them for quite some time, so I touched someone's heart to give them to her for a present."

"So the spiritual does connect to the physical!"

"Yes! Think about it, when Saul went to fight the Philistines they all turned on each other. All my Father had to do was think it and it was so. Who do you think tore down the walls of Jericho? It was my angels."

Now, the Lord asks me if I want to help with the preparations for the Marriage Supper of the Lamb. "Wow!" I quickly exclaimed. "Yes, of course!"

As soon as I agree, I find myself standing in front of a pair of double wooden doors with big gold handles. I walk into a banquet hall filled with tables as far as I can see. These are not just ordinary tables; they are made of very expensive wood. The floors have marble tiles with different colored lines going through each one.

There are white marble pillars all around with windows in between each pillar. I walk over to one of the windows to look outside and see flowers and rose bushes. There is even a place to sit outside. I smell a very strong fragrance like lilac with some other smells mixed in.

Angels are setting plates at each place setting, all with different designs. I ask the Lord about this and He replies, "Each place setting is different because it matches the personality of the person who's going to sit there."

I also notice some angels placing a golden nameplate on each plate while others are taking both the nameplates and the plates away! I asked one of the angels what was going on. He advises me that when a person gets saved, a nameplate is made for him along with the place setting and the wine glass. When that person strays away, or backslides, their place settings are removed and another person takes their place.

I sit down looking at the floor and taking it all in. *I wonder how the Lord feels about all of this.*

"Well, my son, what do you think of the banquet hall?"

"I think it's marvelous, Lord."

"But, my son, now you have to leave I'm afraid."

"Okay, see you later."

Golden Fish

I find myself in heaven by what I call the duck pond. It is located just outside the pearly gates. The reason I call it the duck pond is because I had walked by it previously and noticed Mallard ducks swimming in it. This time I see brightly colored lily pads with some large frogs sitting on top of them, as if sunning themselves. The water is crystal clear. I asked the Lord what do the frogs eat? He said, "Well they don't have to eat anything! Up here in heaven one only eats for the enjoyment of eating. It is the same thing with the animals.

As the Lord was talking I watched a beautiful butterfly land on a frog. At first I thought the frog might eat him, but then the Lord says, "Don't worry my son; no species eats another up here. This particular one has not eaten in a long time. He eats dates, nuts, greens, and the occasional apple. The Lord has a white bowl filled with various foods and throws it into the water. Goldfish come up to eat.

These goldfish are not like the ones you buy in your pet store. I scooped one out with my hand. It must have weighed five pounds and it was bigger than my hand! Its natural coloring was so bright I almost had to cover my eyes! The closest thing I can use to describe it is the scene in the movie *The*

22

Tenth Kingdom when the character played by John Larroquette was traveling on the boat to where they thought the mirror was. Below deck there was a huge goldfish behind a glass frame. John had to break the glass in order to get at it. When he did, he discovered that every-thing the goldfish touched turned to gold. We went on from there; while walking I asked, "Lord, can I go swimming?"

"Immediately I am in what seems to be a park. At one end, there is a lake filled with all kinds of kids playing in the water. Off to one side there is a slide. No, not an ordinary slide. This slide appears to be made of marble, and the ladder's rungs are made of pure gold covered with intricate engravings. I have on a pair of light blue swimming trunks and make a mad dash for the water. Boy, it's so refreshing.

As soon as I have my turn on the slide the Lord tells me it is time to go. Not wanting to hear that I ask why I can't stay, to which He replies, "Because you have more things to do on Earth." So, we hug and I return to my Earth home.

Singing Fountain

I asked the Lord if He could visit me later during the week. He asked, "How about Tuesday?" which is today. I've been looking forward to it. He shows up wearing a light purple shirt with black pants. Wow, He looks marvelous! He walks over to the couch and sits down, drinking a cup of ice cold milk. Go figure.

"Lord, may I have a sip?" He nods, so I take the mug from him. It has a big picture of a white cow on the front. I take a sip and it tastes like no other milk that I have ever tasted. Now He asks, "Do you want to go?"

I immediately reply, "Okay I'm ready." No sooner have I said that, than we are in heaven. We arrive at a three-tiered fountain.

The Lord sits on a bench, watching me. I take a big gulp of water. Wow, that's refreshing! I hear different sounds emanating from different tiers of the fountain as the water cascades down the sides. The middle tier sounds like violins, the bottom sounds like big brass drums, and the top sounds like flutes.

He puts his hand on my shoulder saying, "This fountain sings different tunes all the time."

"Really?"

"Yes, one minute it could sound like all drums, or all flutes, or any instrument." His voice can be so soft and gentle; then other times stern. Just like he talks to a person's heart.

My eyes grow wide at this point as I take a second look at the fountain. It sounds like tambourines and the top tier sounds like trumpets. Then I hear the sound of birds chirping! I exclaimed, "I thought it only played instruments!"

"No, not at all my son."

A good name for it is the singing fountain. The color is an off-white marble; around each edge the tiers have scrollwork. It seemed to be in the middle of heaven.

The Lord says to me, "My son, you have to go now, your time is up." We hug.

Singing Mushrooms

I asked the Lord if I could come up for a visit. He graciously said, "Come on over," meaning He would take time out to visit with me. When my better half gets on the computer she spends hours on it after work. This makes her too tired to go to church. This is how the Devil works. I'm just telling you this to give you a heads up so the same thing won't happen to you. It could be anything, computer games, a hobby, etc. When this happens, just lay it down.

Now, I'm in heaven sitting next to the singing fountain and listening to the music fill my head. My thoughts went to

the movie *The Tenth Kingdom* again. There is a scene where the wicked queen, who represents the Devil, places some singing mushrooms in John Larroquette's way. They started singing some old songs from the 60s. John started to sing along with the mushrooms. As he sang he began getting sleepy until eventually, he laid down for a long nap.

Can you see the similarities of how the enemy works when he lays a trap for you in order to draw you in, a little at a time?

"Lord, how come there are not more people here?"

"People get used to certain things like this fountain until it becomes something they are so used to they scarcely notice it. In heaven it's no different. Once you've been here awhile, or I should say you're a full-timer, you'll see what I mean," He laughingly says.

I'm looking at the water. It seems so inviting, that I just cannot help myself. So, I go for it and jump in! The water feels oh so silky, smooth, and even tastes good. After floating effort-lessly for a while, I turn over and start splashing the Lord. But, to my sheer joy, this time I am able to actually get him wet!

"Hey," He yells, "you're getting me wet!"

As we all know the water dries off quite quickly. I see some rainbows in the water as I watch it cascade down from one tier to another. I could sit here for hours just watching. Every time I come here I see something new.

Now I'm having a big tall glass of moo milk. It is never a small glass and it's always so cold it could give me a brain freeze. The Lord is sipping on a cup of tea with a saucer. He is holding his pinkie finger up just like an old English gentleman, it looks so funny. The Lord then sets his cup and saucer down and says to me "Your time is up, my son."

"Really?" Perhaps I didn't hear him correctly? It always helps when He has a big smile when He says that. We hug and now I'm back.

Bubble Bath

It's nice here in heaven. I'm just walking around; there is no chaperon. No one is around watching me. I can do my own thing. Remember, the Lord had told me that I can come on my own anytime I want! My spirit man knows where heaven is. Right now, I'm standing under my tree house as my mind goes over in the Bible to where it talks about the young prophet and the old prophet in I Kings. After the young prophet had sounded forth a warning against Jeroboam, the Lord told him to depart from the country and to not stop, but go straight home. Sadly, as he was traveling the older prophet met and deceived him, telling him that the Lord said, "It's all right to come with me and feast."

Guess what happened? The young prophet listened to the old prophet instead of the clear word of God. As a result the younger one died before his time when a lion killed him. The old prophet had lied to him! The old prophet in this passage represents people in the church who say "I have a word from the Lord for you." But the message comes from them, not the Lord. The Lord was never involved. *This is what He put in my heart to tell you.*

I'm now at the tree house, the ladder always moves around when I'm climbing up, making it more exciting. You know, come to think of it, I have never seen any ants climbing up and down the tree. If I were on earth I would have to use a ton of bug spray just to keep them at bay. I push open the hatch and look at my dining room. It is then that I notice that despite no one being here for some time there is no dust on any of the furniture! Imagine that.

Next, I go to my bathroom and turn on the hot water. The faucets are the old fash- ioned kind that has separate knobs for the hot and cold water. *Can you wrap your mind around the fact that I have running water with no pipes attached anywhere to the facet!?* The tub is made out of exquisite marble, an off-white color. I forgot to tell you the tub is one of those old- fashioned ones with the claw feet and the high back. The taps are machined pure gold.

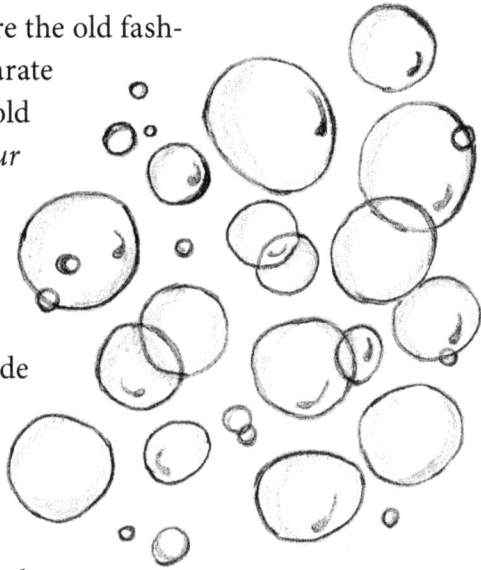

I slip off my clothes and gingerly step in, feeling like a friend coming home. I sink into the water up to my chest. Oh yes, so many bubbles. You have to have bubbles! Now you can only see my head. If I wanted to I could even put my head under the water and stay down for as long as I want. One can breathe underwater here. I don't know how it works, all I know is this is heaven! We are not in the physical, so forget every- thing you have been taught about the "natural laws".

My thoughts drift off into nothingness. The scent of the bubbles fills my nostrils and I let out a joyous laugh. I suspect I have been here for approximately an hour, Earth time. This reminds me of Esther and how the Bible records how she soaked in a tub like this before she went into see the king. Esther soaked for a period of six months. Imagine what would happen to me if I were to soak for one month. I would come out looking like a prune! Ha, ha, we all know that it wasn't six months on a continuous basis.

I haven't seen the Lord at all, or any of his angels. I wonder where everyone is. I get out of the tub, get dressed, and go out to the porch. Still no one in sight! Well, I guess they can trust me now; right? As I turn and walk into my living room there stands one of the Lord's angels! He startles me, because I'm not really expecting to see anyone.

"Well," I blurt out, trying not to sound surprised when in reality I needed a moment to regain a little bit of composure.

"My name is Timothy."

I shake his hand and said, "My name is Richard." But, I know he already knows that.

"The Lord says He has some pressing business to take care of, so He sent me to be your escort. Okay?"

"I really don't need an escort, because as you can see, I'm doing fine."

"That's fine; I just came here to tell you that the Lord can't see you today."

He motions me to come closer and then whispers in my ear "Don't worry, we trust you."

I step back and let out a big, "Hurray!"

"I'll be going then," he says.

"But wait," I catch him just in time.

"Did you know angels can move faster than the speed of light, which is 186,282 miles per second?" he asked me.

I asked him, "How will I know when it's time to go? The Lord usually tells me."

He replies, "Don't worry, you'll know."

Then he's off. I sit down on my couch, trying to digest the conversation that has just taken place. Hmm, I do feel it is almost time for me to be going. My spirit man knows where my home is and takes me there.

Mary

Hmm, it's been too long since I've seen the Lord. If I had a girlfriend she would have called me by now. I hear the Lord saying, "Come up here!" To my surprise, I'm met by Jesus' earthly mother, Mary. I just know who she is. It is an instant recognition. The Lord meets us in the middle of a park setting. I ask the Lord why hasn't He ever introduced me to His mother before? With a smile He replies, "It wasn't time."

Mary looks quite young. She doesn't seem to be much older than a teenager. My curiosity gets the better of me, so I ask her age. She says she is seventeen.

"Were you a shy girl?"

"Yes."

She is petite, standing about 4' 9" slim build, shoulder length hair, brown eyes, and olive colored skin. "Now I know why Joseph married you." She just smiles.

She is wearing normal street clothes—a shirt and pants. I ask her, "How do you like it here?" trying to get her to talk.

"I like it very much, and you?"

"I'm just here part time but it's very nice. At least here you don't have to pay rent on your house!" She smiles in response to my statement. *Boy, I wish she would talk more!*

The Lord answers, "She's okay once she gets to know you."

"Lord, I thought everyone here was perfect and didn't have character flaws."

"My son, everyone has character traits, you'll see this firsthand when you're here full time. But, everyone is still perfect."

We all sit down on a park bench. "Mary," I ask, "What was Jesus like when He was a small boy?"

She laughs. "Oh, He was somewhat mischievous, inquisitive, and always asking questions."

I ask her another question, "Was He weaned at the normal age?"

"Oh yes, there was no problem there. He would go off by himself when He was eight years old. He just wanted to be alone. Most of the kids thought He was illegitimate, because they didn't know the truth, so they made fun of him and talked behind his back. I knew what was going on, but at the same time I couldn't shelter him."

The Lord interrupts, "My son, it's getting late. You have to get up tomorrow, so why don't we finish this discussion some other time."

"Okay Lord," then I shook Mary's hand good-bye; now I'm home.

I meet Mary again a couple of days later. I sit down at my desk in the bedroom when all of a sudden I hear the Lord saying, "Why are you taking soooo looong?"

"I'm just daydreaming."

"I have Mary waiting for you. Don't you want to finish your conversation with her?"

"Oh yes, I'm coming."

Now, we are all in the park again sitting on a bench; just the three of us. *What a great picture that would make!*

"Hi Mary," I offer, shaking her hand and she returns the greeting.

"Mary," I ask right off the bat, "What did you mean when you said, 'Do whatever He asks you to do.' at the wedding in Cana?"

"I was simply voicing that I knew my son was moved by compassion for people's needs, so I knew He would help us. I knew my son's personality while growing up. I also saw the Lord in him.

"How did you handle the criticism of other people around you, especially the other women?"

She looks me in the eyes and responds, "It was very hard when they said, 'She must have had an affair with someone else.' It was very hard. I literally had to run away from them. Sometimes I would just go to Joseph and the two of us would cry. We both went through the scorn and ridicule. When He was first born, they didn't waste any time. The talking started immediately."

She looks at the Lord and smiles. "I knew He was the Savior of the world; the one the prophets of old talked about. I stood up for him many times when people came against him, like when He ate with the sinners. He had compassion for them. They have souls just like you and me."

"Okay," said the Lord, "your time is up."

"Already?"

"Yes, you must be going. I will see you soon."

I say good-bye to Mary then hug the Lord before heading back home.

Chilling out

I sit down to be alone with him. Like so many times before I hear in my spirit, "Would you like to come to heaven now?"

"Sure," I reply, "but can I just chill out?"

He chuckles, "Sure." Now I'm standing beside him, asking if I can go into the countryside and sit down in the tall grass. "Sure," he said again. *Sometimes the Lord is very short on words.*

Now I am somewhere far away from the city. I am sitting on a gentle hillside. Looking around I see hills, trees, grass, and flowers as far as my eyes can see. There is no sun, but everything is as bright as if there were one. I just lie back and close my eyes. I don't sleep, but merely let my mind wander a bit. I can hardly wait until I can do this full-time.

Opening my eyes, I see the occasional butterfly. The Lord comes and sits beside me, putting a piece of grass in his mouth. "Well, my son," He says.

"What?" *He's going to ask me to leave.*

"Oh nothing, just enjoying your company."

"Lord, sometimes I just want to watch everything go by."

"Yeah, I know what you mean."

"Lord, I'm enjoying not doing anything except chilling out.

He looks at me with a twinkle in his eyes. I immediately start looking around. Off in the distance I see a group of large trees. I just know something is there for me, so I get up and start walking in that direction. As I approach the trees I see a swing with a gold bar for a seat and a golden rope that holds the swing to the tree. This is no little rope either; it's thick like a big boat rope. *You will have to see it for yourself.*

The Lord motions me to get on. So, I walk over to the swing and sit down. Gold is a very soft metal so you know the bar had to be pretty thick to hold a normal-sized person. I kicked my feet in order to get the swing started. The gold is quite heavy so I really have to lean into it. I call out to the Lord, "Come on; give me a push!" He goes around behind me and gives me a huge push, sending me flying about five feet in the air.

He gives me another push and now I am going really high. I yell with excitement, "Come on Lord." He just laughs saying, "Okay." Eventually I stop the swing. He sits down beside me and now we both kick our feet at the same time. I yell to the Lord with a giddy schoolboy voice, "I'm going to jump off at the highest point." I launch myself off the swing like a rocket ship but instead of going high into the air I just go far. I don't hurt myself, no one here can get hurt; remember this is heaven.

Now the Lord is slowing down to a stop. He says, "Wow that was rad," as He gives me a high five. It's time my son. I know your body gets tired and now it is quite late on Earth, so you have to go." Sadly, I agree.

"Oh, all right." Like always, I go and give him a hug before going back home.

UFOs

I am in the bathtub when the Lord said, "Are you ready?"

At first I am a little startled that He would ask me during such an awkward time, but I guess that's how relationships are. I'm actually glad because there's something that's been on my mind lately and I wanted to ask him about it.

I have been watching shows about UFOs and Area 51. In fact, the Air Force even conducted an official investigation into UFOs. I really think that rather than being aliens from outer space they are instead the product of children born from the mating of women and fallen angels. It would explain how they are much more advanced than we are and it seems to align with scripture.

One tends to put God in a box by thinking we are the only intelligent beings in the vast ever expanding universe. So, I ask the Lord about it.

"These beings are for real. They don't have a soul, but they do have a spirit. Mankind is the only race I died for on the cross. These beings have been visiting the Earth since long before Roswell."

He takes pleasure in things we don't understand, so I know there is a very good reason. I'm not going to heaven, I changed my mind; but He will come visit me! Now He is here sitting down on my couch, looking splendid as usual.

"Lord, how are you?"

"I'm fine son."

I start chatting right away. I just had to get this UFO stuff off my chest. The Lord then says, "I have to go." We hug each other and say our goodbyes. He leaves just as fast as He comes.

My wife and I had a chat regarding some of the things the Lord had talked to me about. These are some of the points brought up in our discussion. They are very relevant in light of what the various think tanks are proposing. Because the sons of men intermarried with fallen angels their offspring are now flying around in space ships and have been visiting earth for over 2,000 years. The reason the government is trying to cover it up, like they did with Roswell in 1947, is because everything on Earth is geared towards the physical realm. The way you talk, the way you look, the way you carry yourself, etc.

If the government were to acknowledge that other beings have been visiting our planet there would be mass hysteria, because it would be an acknowledgment that there must be a God out there in order to have other life forms. This would give the Devil a very big black eye. This revelation would get people to think outside the box. The Lord said, "Let us make mankind in our image" (Genesis 1:26). We are the only ones to have messed up. Out of all the innumerable worlds throughout the entire universe He died for us.

Pony

I have just returned from my nightly walk. As always, I am asking the Lord when I can come and see him. Now, I find myself walking through the gates. The Lord is on the opposite side just watching people. He's dressed in dark red pants and a light purple shirt. *The color is hard to describe since I have never seen anything quite like it.*

"How are you doing my son?" He shakes my hand vigorously, and motions me to come with him. We start to leave the front gates behind. I asked, "Where are we going?"

He replies, "You'll see." I love it when the Lord surprises me. Now we are in a big field about a mile and half away from the city.

I'm right behind him as we go up one hill and down another. Every once in a while, He stops for me. "I'm not going too fast for you am I my son?"

"Oh no," I reply, "it's just that I'm out of breath!" He stops and abruptly looks at me, "What?"

"Oh Lord, I was just kidding. I had you going for a minute, didn't I?" He just laughed. I guess this is the last hill we are going over because in the distance I see a horse. I make a mad dash for it. It's average sized and light brown in color.

"I know you don't like big horses so I have a medium one for you."

"What do you call him?"

"Nothing until now; why don't you give him a name?"

I attentively watch the horse. "I'll call you Spunk!" I grab a hold of his mane and hoist myself up. "Let's see how fast you can go. Come on, Spunk; let's go!" Hmm, that phrase sounds familiar. We start out slowly, and then as we begin to speed up, I pull gently on his mane. "Come on, Spunk." I can feel the air rushing past my face.

I turn him around just by thinking! I think "Let's go," once again in my mind. Now, we are standing beside the Lord. I jump down saying, "I couldn't have asked for a nicer gift, Lord." I give him a big hug and ask why He likes it way out here away from everyone.

"Spunk's personality is a lot like yours."

"Really!"

"Yes, my son."

"Does he talk?"

"No, my son, he doesn't talk. But, he could if you want him too! Just ask me and he will."

"On second thought don't bother," I told the Lord. "No one would believe that I had a conversation with my own talking horse!" We both laughed. Now it's time for me to go!

Ice Cream

I'm still excited about my horseback ride from a couple of days ago. I asked the Lord if I could go see Spunk, and take him for a ride. The Lord said, "Of course you can." Now I'm in heaven walking towards the grassy hill in the country side. At the top of the hill I see Spunk. I run up to him with the Lord walking behind me. I hop on and cry "Ho." That's all it takes and we're off. Not a fast pace like before, but a steady one.

We turn back towards the Lord who is waiting patiently for us.

"Come on down my son," the Lord said. So I fling one leg over, kind of sitting side saddle as I ease my way down.

"Lord, what does he do when no one is around?"

He said, "Enjoys heaven."

"No byproducts from him right?"

The Lord laughed. "Not from anything in heaven, my son. You don't see any bathroom lines do you?"

"Ah, no Lord."

At this point I had a butterscotch ripple ice cream cone in my hand. It was . . . umm, so good.

The Lord said, "Let me take a bite!" When He did, another scoop of ice cream came back to replace what He had bitten off. I blinked twice, "Wow." He looked at me and laughs, "Yes my son, you saw it right."

"Up until now whenever you ate something you saw it being consumed. Then you got another piece, just like the pie you sometimes eat. Now I'm showing you something different. You are used to it because that's the way it is on Earth, but now you have progressed to where it is automatically replaced if you want more all you have to do is think of it. You actually have a choice to either consume whatever you're eating or have it come back. Newbie's take a while getting used to the concept.

Come with me, I want to show you something." In an instant, we are outside an ice cream shop near a ski slope. We go inside and the first thing I notice is a large number of one gallon tubs of ice cream mounted on the walls. The name of the ice cream is displayed below each tub. Unlike ice cream parlors on Earth there is no freezer case where you pick the flavor you want. A female and a male angel dressed in normal street clothes are there to serve us.

After looking around at the humongous selection available I finally make my choice. "I'll take the chocolate butterscotch ripple please." The female angel asks if I want any toppings. I reply, "Yes, I'll take the butterscotch topping with those little beads on top."

"Very well," and then asks the Lord what He wants.

"I'll take the chocolate chip with chocolate syrup on it."

"Very well I'll be right back." *In case you have ever wondered if there were any female angels in heaven—well, I just got served by one.*

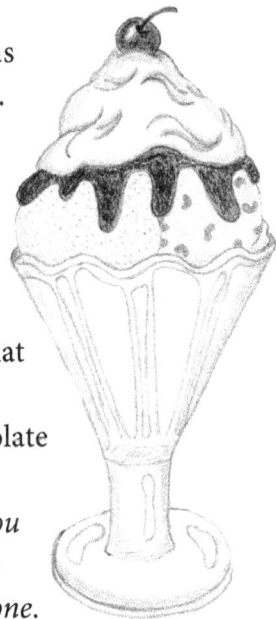

There are different kinds of angels, some with wings, some without. Some angels are only around the throne of the Father. There are warrior angels who fight the Devil and his forces and messenger angels who just go back and forth to Earth to do the Lord's bidding. In fact, angels in heaven do a lot of other things. Maybe I'll share a story just on angels.

After about five minutes she returns with our ice cream. We sit down at a table and quickly dig in. Mine is super delicious. I can't imagine how ice cream can taste so good! I asked the Lord "How's yours?"

"It's fine," He said with a giant smile on his face. After I gulped down the last mouthful, I sit back contentedly. *Not that I was hungry, I just wanted some ice cream.* This was extra special because I got to enjoy it with the Lord!

As we neared the front gates of heaven the Lord turns to me saying, "You have to go now my son." So, I start walking a couple of steps by myself; now I'm back home.

Baseball

I'm in complete darkness in my room, my eyes not really focusing on anything. You guessed it, this was my quiet time. The Lord began saying, "I'm here, where are you?"

"Lord I'm ready now." No sooner had the words left my mouth then I found myself standing next to the Lord near a baseball field. "Lord," I exclaimed, "are we going to have a game?"

"Well, if you would like to join us..."

I'm thinking, who are "us"? Just then I saw about 20 girls and boys all dressed in uniforms with baseball caps and gloves.

"Who's on my team?"

"Why don't you choose someone," the Lord says. "You pick ten and I'll pick ten."

As I pointed to them they said their names and came to stand next to me—Tommy, Allen, Joe, Jane, Tim, Peter, you get the picture. We put our gloves together and shouted, "All for one and one for all! Let's go!" Our team is up to bat first; no coin toss. The Lord is pitching for the other team.

Tommy takes the first bat, a swing and a miss. Even when the Lord is pitching I can see his glory all around Him. Tommy strikes out. Next it is Allen's turn, he strikes out as well. Peter is now up to bat. He swings and misses twice; the third time he connects. You can hear the ball smack the bat. He runs around all the bases; a home run. Hurrah. Next, Tim is up to bat. He swings the bat a couple of times for a warm up and now he's looking straight at the Lord. He swings once, twice, three times—he's out.

Now, the Lord's team is up to bat. I'm the farthest away, in the outfield. John steps up to bat. He's about 6' 4" with a slim build. I hope he doesn't connect! Two swings and a miss; now I'm biting my nails, or glove. He swings the bat back and forth twice, now he's poised. He swings, the bat connects with a crack, the ball sails out of the field.

Now Jennifer is up to bat. She has long blond hair and a slim build. She looks like she could run the bases in eight seconds flat. *I forgot to tell you, Johnny is pitching.* He throws the ball underhanded with a spin on it lifting his leg just like in the major leagues. Jen swings, bam! The ball comes straight toward me in a perfect arch. I catch it.

Our team is up by one, but now the Lord is up to bat! He hits the bat against his shoes. A swing and a miss. The second pitch is also a swing and a miss. I guess He hasn't played this game in over two thousand years. Finally, on the third pitch He connects. You could hear the smack a mile away. The ball goes higher and higher. No one is able to see it, let alone catch it. The final score is 2 to 1. We lost, but we had a lot of fun.

I shake everyone's hand and then have a cold one . . . a glass of milk. Hey, this is heaven after all. We are still at the baseball field when the Lord tells me that I have to go now.

A Cheer Up

I really miss the Lord. Sensing my thoughts, He answers, "You may come to my kingdom; come on up, my son."

I'm now standing beside a merry-go-round. I don't know if it's the same one as before. This one has a bright red horse. The Lord says "Come on, please get on. I think you need some cheering up!"

"Yeah Lord, you're right."

Everyone here is so happy. I know that if I wasn't part time I wouldn't need cheering up. He rides beside me on a blue horse. It has a black saddle that matches its mane. These horses go up and down. The other merry-go-round never did that. I'm beginning to cheer up as I watch the Lord riding a horse on a merry-go-round.

The merry-go-round stops and we get off. He puts his arm around me and asks if I feel better. I reply, "Oh yes Lord, I'll be okay." Now I find myself sipping on an iced tea.

"You know you only have one real home my son; it's here with me in heaven. You're just a visitor on Earth."

"Lord, I just want to spend time with you instead of just going here and there."

"Would you like to go to your tree house? We could sit on the couch and just chill!"

"Oh yeah, that would be fun Lord."

Now we are sitting on my porch with two glasses of a soda-like drink. I put my feet on a chair in front of me. He takes my hand saying, "Isn't this nice?"

"Yeah, it really is! Lord, it has been nice even though we didn't do very much and I'm not so sad anymore." We hug. He says goodbye and now I'm back.

Cinderella

It's been a ho-hum day with nothing special going on. All I'm doing is watching the last few days of the Olympics. Only a couple of the medal winners bothered to thank the Lord out of the hundreds who were given them. It makes one wonder if just maybe the rest thought they won by the power of their own strength. I hear the Lord saying "Don't you see the rain falling? As you worship me blessings come down from above. Let me take you to a higher realm in me as my rain continues to fall. It saturates the ground and the waters begin to rise."

"First it reaches your ankles, then your waist, and eventually it's over your head. The reason the people drowned during Noah's time was they didn't want any part of me! In order for people to save themselves they're going to have to depend totally on me as the water rises around them."

The Lord asks me if I want to go to heaven. I say, "Yeah maybe, just kidding." I meet him at the front gates again; I guess it must be one of his favorite meeting places, just like the singing fountain. He walks up to me "How are you?"

"I'm fine. What's going on?"

"Oh nothing much, just regular stuff; you know, making sure everything is set for the big day." Yeah is all I can think

50

to say. I know He can't go into detail about kingdom stuff. "You're right my son," He says laughing. He just read my thoughts again.

"Here, have a milkshake on me!"

I offer him a sip and He shakes his head and motions with his hands, no thanks. The two of us are watching people's faces as they walk through the gates for the first time. Even though I have done this before I never get tired of it.

I would like to share a story that the Lord has put on my heart if you don't mind. My wife and I had just arrived back in the states from the Philippines. We were there on All Saints Day, which is similar to Halloween.

What families do is go to the local cemetery where their loved ones are buried. Once there, they light candles and pray for the loved one to enter heaven. Afterward they eat lunch or dinner on top of the person's grave. I witnessed thousands and thousands of people there. Some families even stay overnight. Some Catholic priests wearing white robes give their blessings to the people.

I ask the Lord what He thinks about all of this. He just shakes his head in sorrow and says, "My word clearly states that one has to be born again in order to enter heaven's gates. Once they are dead it is too late. They have already made their choice."

I turn to the Lord, getting tired of looking at people for the moment. "Lord, you know Christmas is just around the corner, so what are you going to give me?" He laughed just like Santa. "You'll see." I look real serious at him. "Yes my son, it's a real nice present." Wow! I thought of all the nice things He could give me.

"My son, you have to go now."

"Really," I said, "you must have the wrong person!" He pulls out a piece of paper that looks like a plane ticket and continues, "Boarding is Richard Smith departing at 11 PM Seat # 7 aisle 7; window seat."

I laugh. Then I see two white horses coming around the corner pulling a coach. It isn't like the stagecoaches featured in the old westerns. Instead it is completely round just like Cinderella's. It comes at us at a fast pace before stopping right in front of me. Two angels are in the drivers seats. It looks similar to what you see after you peel an orange. You see ridges or pulp all around. There are four ridges from top to bottom on the stagecoach looking like an orange gold in color.

It has four big wagon-like wheels with the outside rim as clear as glass. The spokes are the same color as the four ridges. The coach is radiant, an off-white, and has two doors in the middle with ornate curved gold handles at each end. The doors are made of dark wood.

One of the angels steps down and opens the door. Immediately a step made of pure gold came out from underneath. I am greeted by red velvet seats; in fact everything is red velvet inside. As I sit down I look up to notice a young girl sitting opposite me. This takes me by surprise because I expected to be the only passenger. She is beaming and looks like Cinderella. She is wearing a blue ruffled dress and has blonde, shoulder length hair, light blue eyes, and a light complexion. I put out my hand and say, "Hi, my name is Richard." She responds, "My name is Kate." I notice her dimples as she smiles. *I wish she really was Cinderella.*

"Well Kate, what brings you here today?"

"The Lord approached me the other day and asked if I wanted to take a ride to Earth. I said yes, of course."

"Do you get people who ask if you are really Cinderella?"

"Yes all the time, but they are mostly people who haven't been here long," she laughs with a slightly red face. I hear the

Lord saying to the angels "Take him by the snowy mountains, he'll like that." Very good was their reply, then off we go.

The mountains come up quickly and I realize we must be traveling at an amazing speed. It feels like we turn to the right and are descending. I look out the window and see the Earth fast approaching. I glance at Kate who is looking out on her side, watching all of this. As we exit the clouds I notice the ground coming up to meet us. Now, we are just above the trees and I'm going through the roof of my house.

I look at Kate. She smiles as I ask her if I will ever see her again.

"I'll be around, just keep your eyes peeled for me." We shake hands and the doors open. I step down from the coach and into my bedroom; the stagecoach is off in a split second.

Alone

This happened early on when I first started visiting with the Lord in 2009, just before I went to have an operation. I knew that I had to have it, still, in my mind I didn't want to go through with it. What if something went wrong?

The Lord didn't feel like going to the cross that day, but He knew He had to. I wasn't really relishing the thought of how much pain I would be in after the surgery. The Lord had this to say, "You will be fine. It can't hurt as much as when they pulled out my beard or when they started hitting me in the face with their fists while I was blindfolded and mocked me, asking me to tell them who hit me."

"They hit me in the ribs countless times, thinking if they could make my muscles sore and bruised it would be much harder for me to breathe. Because they were hitting me in the face they also knocked out some of my teeth. They hit me so hard my teeth punctured my cheeks and dug into my lips. They were one of the first things cut and swollen because of all of the beating.

"Some of my gums were bleeding, causing my mouth to quickly fill up with blood. Mixed with saliva some of it dropped down my swollen cheeks and onto my chest. The rest

I was forced to swallow which, along with my broken nose, made it even harder to breathe. These soldiers were not wimps. They were the fiercest warriors Rome had ever produced and when they marched the world trembled. They even stomped on my feet, trying to break my toes!

"The crown of thorns did not come from a rose bush. They were several inches long and it was rammed down onto my head in a deliberate attempt to force the thorns to pierce my brow. This punctured blood vessels in my scalp causing warm blood to flow into my eyes, running down my hair and into my ears.

"I could see very little for my eyes were almost swollen shut because of the many fists hitting me. Any normal man would have hemorrhaged and died right there from the loss of so much blood. They hurled all the sarcasm and insults they could think of, while they pummeled me with their fists. Then they put one of my robes back on me simply to let the blood coagulate on the sores before ripping it off in delight, making me bleed once more. As they waited for the blood to coagulate they continued to insult me.

"This was even before they flogged me with the cat of nine tails. The soldier with the whip weighed over 200 pounds. He had a smile on his face even before he hit me the first time!

Since my eyes were nearly swollen shut, all I could do was hear the sound of the man with the whip saying "Okay then," even so, the crowds were still jeering. The first shock of the whip hurt the most. I knew what was coming so I tensed up.

"I endured all 39 lashes. The pieces of bone, glass, and pottery on the ends cut into my flesh, ripping off deep chunks that exposed my bone. In the process it also pulled out some of my already matted hair, and shredded my muscles in the process. The whipping wasn't confined to just my back, the ends of the lash would go up my neck and even my ears and shoulders.

"As I walked up the path to Golgotha I looked at the crowds that had formed. Some were crying, some were mocking me, and others were jeering. Yet some had sorrowful expressions on their faces. Some even spat on me as I passed by; but I forgave them. The blood that had filled my ears started to coagulate so I couldn't hear the noise of the crowds. I stumbled along the way from the constant hitting, plus the pain in my ears caused my equilibrium to be off.

"As I continued to walk I found it harder to breathe. I found myself gasping for air because some of the blood dried up in my nose, so my mouth was the only way for me to get any oxygen. Even that was agonizingly difficult for my mouth was still swollen from the beating, and then there was the added weight of the cross.

"I'm glad my father arranged for Simon to be right where he was, so he could carry the cross the rest of the way up the hill. By the time I got to the end of my walk my feet had almost no insteps. Because of the swelling my body spasmed in pain as they drove the spikes mixed with dirt and blood into my feet and wrists.

"Many people think the spikes they used were put in the palms of my hands, but the Romans had perfected the art of crucifixion. They precisely placed the spikes just above the wrists where the surrounding bones would be strong enough to hold a man's weight. I was glad because I knew the end was in sight; everything was nearly finished."

"Just as there were many who were appalled at him, his appearance was so disfigured beyond that of any man, and his form marred beyond human likeness" (Isaiah 52:14).

After He said all this He asked if I would still like to come and spend some time with him. I said respectfully, "No Lord. I have had enough for now." I had to digest what I had just heard.

Walking on Water

I was glad when I finished the day at work; it had dragged on and on. I hear the Lord saying, "Come on." Up in heaven I run up and give him a big kiss. "How are you, my son?"

"I'm tired from work Lord, but I'm here. I want to spend some time with you before I go to bed." Now, the two of us are walking hand-in-hand outside the front gates.

"I want to show you something. There are some trees just beyond the gates," the Lord said pointing to them. "Let's go over there." We take our time walking. Once we get there I notice that they are apple trees.

"Lord, I thought all the trees are in a different part of heaven."

"Well my son, they could be anywhere."

"Yeah, you're right," I said, picking an apple from the first tree I see. Ummm, it is so sweet! Wow!

"Here my son, try this one." He takes one off the tree and I am stunned. It is sweeter than the one I just had. "Good?" He asked. "Yeah," I blurted out as pieces of apple fell out of my mouth. I looked over and spy some orange trees. The oranges are the size of grapefruits. I peel one and all I can say is "Wow!" again.

"I thought you would like them."

"Oh yes, Lord, I really like them." We started walking again. "Lord can we go over there?" I asked, pointing to the vast green fields beyond.

"Sure, let's go for a walk."

We proceed to walk to the fields. "Lord, do you see what they are doing to me at work?"

"Yes my son, soon you'll be leaving this job. It has almost outlived its usefulness for my purposes. You have learned many lessons while employed there."

"Yes Lord, you're right."

I have a drink in my hand. It makes me feel a bit better. Walking by some trees I suddenly get a notion to climb one. Have you ever climbed a tree when you were young? In heaven it's very easy, not like on Earth where you have to struggle. I wave to the Lord. I feel like Zacchaeus when he climbed the Sycamore tree to see the Lord. After I jump down the Lord says, "Come on I want to show you something." The next thing I know we are standing at the duck pond just outside the front gates. "Watch," He says as we approach it. He starts to walk upon the surface of the water. Wow, I thought this only happened when you were on Earth.

"Now, it's your turn, my son." I walk right up to the water's edge and put one foot on the surface. Amazingly it doesn't go down! I put more weight on it and I'm still not going down. Wow this is great. I'm about to explode from all the excitement! Soon I have two feet standing on top of the water. I look down, trying to see the goldfish. I yell to the Lord who is watching from the bank. "Look Lord I'm standing!"

He laughs as I begin to take baby steps at first. Eventually I feel more confident to where I start walking faster and now I'm running!

I'm so excited I run as fast as I can over to the Lord. *What would happen if I were to treat it like ice. I'll run and then see if I can slide!* I call out to the Lord, "Watch this!" I start running as fast as I can and then put on the brakes and start sliding as if I was on ice! I don't know how it works, but this is what's happening. I look at the Lord and He is laughing like Santa again. I like making him laugh.

He says, "My son, you give me great pleasure. Don't sell yourself short my son; you are mighty through me. I want you to see yourself in your heavenly attire because that's who you truly are! Now let's go over to your place for a while."

In a split second, I'm at home waiting for the Lord to arrive. As I'm sitting on the floor with my back against the couch the Lord just walks through the living room wall. I see gold in the air all around him. It's his glory.

He sits down on the couch and crosses his legs. I get up from the floor and sit beside him, putting my arm around him. He smiles. *You have to have a good relationship with the Lord in order to put your arms around him.* "Lord," I ask, "can I put my head on your lap?"

"Sure, my son." I move down to the very end of my couch and put my head on his lap. He begins running his fingers through my hair, He knows I like that. "Lord, how do you know all the stars by name, don't you forget them?"

"No" He said. "I named all of them. It's like Adam; he named all the animals, right?"

"Yes, Lord."

"And he didn't forget any."

"Lord, why is it that some people pray a lot to you and you answer them right away, while at other times it seems to take forever?"

"It's all in the timing my son. Take you for instance. Haven't you been asking me about certain things for over 30 years?"

"Yes, Lord."

"But it's all about timing. If I had given you all that I had in mind 30 years ago you would not have been able to handle it, so you see what I mean."

"Yes Lord, I understand now."

I'm still lying down at this point. "Well my son, I have to be going now."

"But Lord, you just got here!"

"Yes my son, I know. But, I have things to do to make preparation for my bride which will come to me soon."

"I understand, so I'll see you later okay." Then He just vanished.

Ice Rink

I take a refreshing drink from the water. I see the Lord walking towards me as I enter heaven.

"How are you doing my son?"

"I'm fine, Lord. Can you take me ice skating, please?"

"What makes you think I have an ice rink here in heaven?"

I just looked at him, "Well do you?"

He laughs. "I'll take you there myself."

I find myself standing at an ice rink, but it doesn't have any Christmas lights or any type of decoration. I ask the Lord about it. "The reason is because it's always Christmas up here."

"Well Lord that makes since, but you know I still like all the Christmas stuff." He just laughs.

The rink is in the middle of a field surrounded by benches. There are no lights for night skating. It has boards all around the perimeter. There is no glass around and no penalty box. Basically it's like an old fashioned rink. Angels are serving drinks at one end of the rink. I walk over ask for some hot chocolate, even though it's not cold. Then, I walk over to where the Lord is standing.

"Lord," I ask, "can I try on a new pair of skates? You know, like the ones they have on Earth."

"Yes, of course."

We then sit down on one of the benches and He picks up a box with a ribbon on it. I exclaimed, "You didn't!"

"Open it."

I rip off the wrapping paper. If you really want to know the color, the paper is red with gold inlay and the bow is bright red. I open the top and inside is a pair of brand new skates. Wow! When I was growing up I never could afford a brand new pair, this is so fantastic!

"Try them on."

The skates are black on the outside. The material seems like leather and the inside is perfectly formed to my feet. The blades are shiny gold. "Forgive me for asking."

"Yes, my son?"

"Can I have the clear gold blade instead of the colored one?"

He laughs, "Are you sure?"

"Yes I am sure." I look at the skates again and sure enough the blades are clear gold! Gold, but no color. Only in heaven could this be possible.

I push the tongue down and am about to lace them up, admiring them as I turn them from side to side when before my very eyes they laced themselves up in a split second. *I wish I could make something on Earth that would do that, not only for skates but all kinds of shoes.* I give the Lord a big hug, Lord they mean a lot to me. He ruffles my hair, "You're welcome, it's my pleasure." I jump on the ice and away I go. I'm not the only one on the ice there are about twenty-five other people out here.

The rink is big so there's a lot of space for everyone. I twirl and jump, just like an Olympic skater, even better because everything is so perfect. I do a triple sow cow then spin and land on one skate. After about half an hour I skate over to the Lord, checking on my time! He says, "You have about five more minutes."

I say, "Ten!"

He answers, "Fine", and away I go again. *I love skating it's so relaxing.* I skate over to the Lord again.

"Time is up my son, time to come in."

"Okay," I say and I walk off the ice rink. *The ice is not cold to the touch plus you didn't need a Zamboni to clear it.*

When I walk off the ice, I suddenly notice my skates are already undone. I put on my shoes and ask, "Where to now?" hoping He would change his mind about me going.

"I'm sorry, my son, you have to be going now."

"Really?"

"Yes, I'm afraid so." I give him a big hug and start walking way.

Skateboarding

I t's nearing Christmas, my favorite time of the year. Singing Christmas carols, generally people are in better moods at this time of year, and spending lots of money on presents. I hear the Lord saying in my heart.

It's sad, very sad. Yes there are some who think more of me during Christmas than at any other time of the year. Soon after people celebrate the New Year and reflect on the things they have done over the past year. Some experience regrets while others want to draw closer to me. It will be a time for gathering together in one mind and one body.

I go to meet the Lord at the front gates. It really is like Christmas here all the time. People are smiling, happy, and laughing; there is so much love flowing from everyone. This is unheard of on Earth.

The Lord is wearing light Khaki colored shorts with a dress shirt and sandals. I run up to him and give him a big hug. He asks me "Are you good?"

"Yeah I'm good now." I see the mountains in the distance so I ask the Lord if we can go there. When asked why, I answer, "Just because?"

"Sure, I don't see why not." So, I start to move up into the atmosphere like someone was pulling me up. Now I'm standing close to the top of one of the peaks. It has a lot of snow, so I expect it to be cold, but I don't feel it. *On earth you know it's really cold when you can see your breath, but it's not even that cold!*

I look down at a ridge and see two mountain goats about a mile away. They're beautiful, majestic with big long horns and white snowy fur coats. I ask, "Lord, why do you have mountain goats up here in heaven?" I don't have to be beside him to talk to him.

The Lord answers me, "It gives me pleasure to watch them."

Now I'm transported to the front gates again. The Lord continues, "Just like humanity my son, it gives me pleasure watching them. I know that concept is hard for you to understand because you're not infinite like me, looking at the beginning and the end at the same time."

***

I see a person riding a bike from the 1800s with a big wheel at the front and a smaller one in the back. He winks at me as he passes by. Now, I have a foot-long hot dog in my hand. I wash it down with a tall cold glass of milk. For dessert, I'm having a big slice of banana cream pie. I turn to the Lord. I'm having so much fun, it feels like Disney World. Now, I see three or four people on skateboards.

"Lord, I've never been on a skateboard; can I try it?"

"Yes, sure my son."

Instantly I see one at my feet. It's gold with the appearance of clear plastic, just like the ice skates. The gold is quite heavy, having the regular thickness of a skateboard. It has a picture of a white flying eagle, with gold lettering. The outside edges have a thin gold line all around. The wheels are solid gold with a lighter color on the inside where they attach to the housing.

How on Earth am I going to get a good ride if the wheels aren't made of rubber? I spin one of the wheels. To my aston- ishment, it spins very smoothly and just keeps on spinning. I wish I could market this on Earth!

"Yes, my son," the Lord laughs. "We build whatever you can think of because up here everything is made to perfec- tion." The underside of it has a gold plate that reads 11, 25, 11. The plate has three rubies on each side. The numbers are the time it was given to me.

I notice that my clothing has changed. I am wearing short pants with a black and white striped t-shirt and black running shoes. I yell out to the Lord, "I'm off!" I give two pushes and already I am going super-fast. I am passing people on bikes! I have never had so much fun before. I go about five miles along the main drag and back again to where the Lord is standing.

"Lord I really like my skateboard. It's beautiful, thank you so very much."

"You're welcome my son. I knew you would like it."

It's nice to hear the Christmas music at the holiday season. I wish they could play it when it's not Christmas. I want to get to know the Lord more so I'm spending a lot more time with him. *Just like you and your spouse if you're married. Remember when you first started dating? He or she was all you could think about. Then after so many years of marriage you kind of slacked off. I don't want that to happen with the Lord and me.*

"Can we sit on a park bench for a while?"

"Very well." Now, we are sitting on a bench with trees all around. The temperature is perfect and best of all there are no mosquitoes.

"Lord, I love this place! I mean the park and stuff."

"Yes, my son, it's quite nice." I lay my head on his legs as I stretch out on the bench.

He runs his hands through my hair. *Boy that feels nice.* Now I hear the Lord as He starts singing to me. "We are one my son, we are one. Just like a school boy and his dog they are inseparable, like a tongue licking a stick of candy."

I say in a dreamy voice, "Lord, that was so peaceful."

I sit up and a blue bird lands on my shoulder. After a few moments he flies off, and then a big butterfly lands on my hand. I just bounce my hand up and down, watching his wings move.

During all of this the Lord just sits there watching everything. Now a little girl comes over to us and hugs him. I asked her, "Don't I get a hug?" She comes over and gives me one too. "Well my son," the Lord starts to say. "Time is moving on and I have a lot of work to do."

"Lord, can I help you?"

He laughs and said "No, but when you come here full time you can. You have to go now, my son. It's getting late."

"Yeah, I know." I get up and give the Lord his goodbye hug; now I'm back.

Hospital Visit

The Lord is waving his hands at me as if He were guiding an aircraft in for landing. He's asking where I want to meet him. I reply, "A bench in a park, Lord."

"Okay." Now I'm sitting beside him. He's wearing a dark red long sleeve shirt with white dress pants and black leather shoes.

"Wow, you look magnificent!" I blurt out.

"Well, thank you son, do you want an outfit like this one?"

"Really?" I said loudly. "Yes, of course." I give him a big hug and when I let him go I find myself wearing a short sleeve shirt just like the Lord's red one.

The Lord slaps me on the knee. "I'm so glad to see you, my son. I've missed you!"

"Me too, Lord."

"Where would you like to go, my son?"

"Lord, I would like you to take me to a Hospital in Vancouver, British Columbia to pray for people." I don't know why I said that! I guess it was on the Lord's mind.

"Are you sure, my son? Well get ready." With that He stands up, grabs my hand, and immediately we are standing in front of a nursing station at a hospital in Canada.

There are four nurses behind the desk, all looking at computers. I see other nurses coming and going.

A piece of paper on a clipboard reads "Vancouver Hospital." *I have never been to Vancouver before so perhaps I should go on a short sightseeing tour while I am here. Maybe one of the nurses could take me.*

I turn and look to my right; a sign above the door to the stairs says, Third Floor. "Okay Lord, where to?"

"Can they see us?" He says, "No", and then points to my right. "Let's go this way." It smells like the floor has just been polished. As I'm following the Lord down the hall a couple of people walk right through us and keep on walking. I wish I had my skateboard; it would fit right in on the newly waxed floor! Especially since no one would see me.

"In here," says the Lord and we go into room 305. The room has a single sleeping occupant connected to a heart monitor. I ask the Lord what's wrong with him. He told me the man was in a car accident and has some internal bleeding. They will need to operate in order to close the wounds.

"If we wake him up will he see us?"

"Yes my son, this is the exciting part when people actually see us; from the spiritual to the physical. The expression on their faces always stays in your mind. Sometimes they ask all kinds of questions.

I'm standing on one side of the bed and the Lord is on the other. The Lord says to me, "When he opens his eyes he will see us."

"I will remove the scales from his eyes. Ready?"

"Yes Lord," I say as I shake the side of the bed. The man doesn't respond, so I rock it a second time, saying, "Wake up."

His eyes pop open, and he stares at us as if we had two heads. As he tries to sit up, I say softly, "Here let me help you." I get a pillow and put it behind his back.

He asks, "Who are you and how did you get in here?" I laugh and tell him we just popped in. He looks us over and then turns to the Lord and suddenly exclaims, "Jesus, Lord Jesus, praise you Jesus!"

"So, you're Mike?" I ask.

"Yes, but how do you know my name?"

"I just know. I would like to lay my hands on your mid-section in order for you to be healed in His name." I point to the Lord sitting on the end of the bed. Mike nods his head.

I put one hand on his mid-section, then holding one hand up I say, "Father, let this bleeding stop right now. I proclaim it in Jesus' name, and it is so. Amen."

As I remove my hand he says, "I felt a burning sensation when you prayed."

"Now you're good to go! You don't need to have that operation anymore."

He grabs my hand and with tears running down his face, he cries, "Thank you." The Lord gives him a hug too. He's so excited that he is beside himself. He pushes the call button and cries out, "Nurse; Nurse." Responding to his frantic voice a pair of nurses rush in and ask what's wrong.

"I don't have to have that operation. I'm healed." One of the nurses took him by the hand in an attempt to calm him down.

"Tell your doctor in the morning and see what he says, okay?" Mike kept on telling them to let the doctor know that he didn't need the surgery. One of the nurses comes back in the room with a small white pill saying, "Here Mike, take this. It will help you sleep."

He takes it with some water then looks at me and the Lord. "Thank-you for coming."

Just then the Lord says to me "It's time, my son, you have to go now."

"Yeah," I reply and hug the Lord. Then turn to Mike saying, "Goodbye."

Trip to Switzerland

"Come my son," I hear the Lord saying and in an instant I find myself in heaven. Sitting in the middle of a park the Lord asks me, "Where would you like to go?" My head is still spinning, everything is happening so fast. *Wow, he's really asking me. I'd better think real hard, hmm.*

"Lord, I would like to go someplace I have never been before!"

He gets up from the park bench. "I have just the place, hold my hand." Now, I find myself flying though space back down to Earth.

"Lord, I've just come from Earth! I was hoping to be somewhere . . . like another planet!"

He chuckled, "I know," and I now find myself in Switzerland! I know this because I see a sign that says "Welcome to Switzerland" on a mountain road.

Taking a quick look around I see a lot of mountains up close. I blurt out, "Let's go to a village." Now we are standing in front of a restaurant with tables outside in the front. The temperature feels about 64 degrees. The server comes out and asks us if we would like a menu. I look at the Lord and He replies, "No thanks, we'll have the cheese cake and coffee please."

"Lord," I whisper, "how are we going to pay for it, he sees us."

"Don't worry, I've got it covered, everyone sees us here, unlike some places we visit where only certain people see us," the Lord whispers back.

The server comes out in a couple of minutes with our coffee and cheese cake. Both of them are just exquisite. I start to look around. There's a bar at one end with about twenty different kinds of beer on tap. The streets aren't quite as wide as we're used to in America and it seems the shops are mostly made of old-fashioned bricks. The majority of the people are wearing light jackets.

The server comes out with our check; it's $10.50. The Lord reaches into his breast pocket and pulls out some money. We leave and proceed to walk down the main street. It has a lot of shops. Some of them are selling fancy glass vases and colored dishes. The time is getting short for this visit, so the Lord says, "I have to go." I ask Him if I can stay here on my own and He tells me of course, but some other time.

"My angel will escort you." As He says that a big angel suddenly appears beside me. I hug the Lord, and now I'm off. We fly way above the Earth so high I can see the entire continent of North America. Now we are going down at breakneck speed. Just before we get to the roof of my home we suddenly slow down as we pass through and end up back inside. The angel left me there and in the blink of an eye he was gone again.

Book of Life

I'm here in my living room where I have just closed my eyes, concentrating on the Lord when I see two angels He assigned to me, standing in my living room. Everyone has angels assigned to them. I also see my diamond sandals. I know I don't see these things often enough, which is something I have to work on more. I don't see my sandals in the natural realm, only in the spiritual realm. Someday by faith they will appear in the physical.

Now I hear the Lord asking if am ready for a visit. I quickly respond, "Yes, I sure am." Now I'm here just outside the city gates. I wave "Hi" to the two angels who are always there with the *Book of Life*. I walk up and ask if I can sit there and look at the *Book of Life* for a moment. They looked at each other and then at the Lord. He nodded okay. I have described the front gates but never really paid much attention to the book before.

I sit down at the desk where the book is resting. It looks to be about 12 x 12 inches and about 4 inches thick. The cover is gold inlaid with scrolls along the outer edges. The pages have scrolls on the outer edges and it says in bold gold letters "*The Book of Life.*"

As I turn the first page I notice it is thick and crinkly. You get the impression that if you were to bend it the wrong way it would break off. But, as I look at the page while turning it the whole book seemed to be alive. As I turn to the fifth page, for no particular reason I stopped and looked at the names listed in alphabetical order, last name first. As I run my finger down the page, I notice some of the names disappearing while others appear in their place. I ask the Lord about this and He explains, "My son, it's just like the plates on the tables for the Marriage Supper. The angels are always taking and removing names at the same exact moment. When this happens they are also taken and removed from the *Book of Life*."

I realize that makes perfect sense. "Lord can I look for my name?" He told me to go ahead, so I keep turning until I reach the "S" section. Just like a phone book, there are a lot of Smith's. He chuckles. My finger was tired from going through page after page, but I finally find it. Smith Richard, July 3rd, 1973, 2:45 pm. Then it had a space for notes below.

The angel clears his voice, loudly hinting it was time for me to get up. I thank him for letting me see. He smiles at me and says it's quite okay, and sits down again. Now, the Lord comes up to me and asks where I want to go as He puts his arm around me.

"You know Lord, I just like it when you put your arm around me. I just love it when you show your love to me. And in your word it says if I have left land and houses for your sake I will have it given to me in this life. Lord I'm still waiting!"

"Yes my son, I don't lie. It's coming, so don't give up."

"Lord," I respond. "Can I go now? I'm really tired. I had a hard day at work."

"See you later, my son."

Strange Flowers

The Lord is faithful. We may have to go through a season in order to get to where the Lord wants us to be, but in the end we will make it. The Lord gave me work last week through an employment agency. I don't know how long it will last, but it's a means to an end. Now I hear the Lord. "Come on I'm waiting for you."

I'm glad he's waiting for me. Now I'm just outside of the front gates again. The air is fresh, like what you smell during an early morning walk in the countryside.

I see the Lord walks towards me from the other side of the gates. He is smiling, which is a good thing. He greets me by saying, "How are you, my son?" and shakes my hand. "I'm fine," I reply. He immediately puts His arm around me, and we start walking away from the gates. I glance back as we begin our walk.

We walk by the duck pond. I run up to it, looking to see if any fish are at the surface. No such luck. The Lord says, "They are at the bottom." We start walking along the pathway again. I never get tired of looking at all the vibrant colors here. It's like a scene out of the Disney film *Mary Poppins* where they jump into the picture and end up in another place where everything is vibrant and exciting. But here in heaven, I'm afraid to say, there is no animation; at least not that I have seen.

He has on his white robes with a blue scarf around his neck, so naturally I ask him "Why are you wearing your robes?"

He smiles saying, "I just wanted to wear them today that's all. No big deal." I just look at him. Up ahead I see a whole lot of flowers. I run over to a bright yellow flower, I'm not sure what the variety is.

I smell it without even thinking. It smells like butterscotch candy, amazing! The Lord asks me, "Why don't you have a taste?" I look at him, digesting what He just said. I know heaven is different, but flowers you can eat!? Okay, I'll try it, I hear myself say. I bite off the top half of a flower. It really tastes the way it smells! The more I bite down, the more the flavor fills my mouth.

I look at the Lord. I can tell he's really enjoying this. I pull one of the petals off and put it into my mouth. It tastes like peppermint! Wow, the top is butterscotch and the bottom part is peppermint.

My mind is on tilt. I'm trying to understand what just took place. I assumed that the entire flower would be butterscotch. I look at the Lord and He's laughing like Santa Claus again. He's even making me laugh. After He calms down a bit He says, "The look on your face is priceless."

"Well Lord, you got me this time."

We continue to walk when all of a sudden an angel walks up to the Lord and says something and is gone. He turns to me saying, "I have some kingdom business to attend to, so you have to be going now, but thank you for spending time with me. It was very enjoyable." We hug and now I'm home again.

Fields of Flowers

Heaven is my only place of refuge. I see too many disturbing things going on down here on Earth, but I know the Lord is still on the throne. He has a place for those who love him. I can hardly wait! When I'm full-time I think I will just stay in my tree house. Just kidding, I know we will rule and reign with him. Life on Earth is too short. You're lucky if you make it to 85 or 90. That is short, it's just a short visit compared to eternity.

The word of God says our life is like chaff that gets blown away in the wind and is no more. So do what the Lord asks of you, for only what is done for his kingdom will remain. I hear the Lord saying, "Come on."

I find myself in a field of daffodils with all manner of beautiful colors. These are not little fields, they are huge. I guess the Lord really likes flowers. I just flop on my back, taking in all the wonderful fragrances.

An occasional bee or butterfly passes by, not small ones either. If you could just see what I see; it is mind boggling. Come to think of it, I don't even have to walk to the next field I just think of it and I am there. The Lord walks over to me saying "Hi my son, I see you're enjoying yourself." I just nod; I'm at a loss for words. It is overwhelming!

All of a sudden, an angel appears, standing beside me. He's wearing white robes, no warrior gear on, but he has wings on his back. I ask him if I can touch them. He says, "Sure," then he turns around. I start at the top and work my way down. The feathers are soft to the touch, but are held firmly in place.

He says, "Why don't we run through the fields together, it will be fun." Wow, this is the first time an angel has asked me to do something with him other than taking me home.

"Okay, let's go." I take hold of his hand letting him know I'm ready. Now, we are both running through the daffodils. I notice that when we step on them they just spring back up. The same thing happens with the grass. We run about two miles without stopping. I look back and see the Lord talking with an angle way off in the distance.

The angel comes over to me and informs me he will be escorting me home. He asks, "Are you ready?"

"Yes," and that was all I was able to get out before I land in my bedroom. I see him for a split second longer and then he is gone.

Loved Ones

I asked the Lord earlier in the week if I could spend some quality time with him. This particular day I just walked into my room and was not even thinking about the Lord, when all of a sudden I hear "I'm ready whenever you are." Now I'm in heaven. I really like my new home here. It's so much nicer than my house on Earth.

Nothing is ever the same in Heaven, things are always changing and there are always new things to experience. I'm at the front gates, *in case you're wondering,* and the Lord is waiting for me. He smiles as He walks towards me. I give him a big hug saying, "Oh Lord; Master. I missed you so very much, I really have."

He looks lovingly at me saying, "You know, I feel the same way. Let's go over here a ways." We go along to a grassy spot and then down a hill to what seems to be another park setting. It has a small pond with some big oak trees surrounding it.

"Here, have a seat, my son." I sit down on the grass, no blanket required. I exclaimed, "I haven't been on a picnic in a very long time!"

"I have a surprise for you!" Just then I see my cat Ming-Ming. *To remind you, he was the cat my wife and I used to*

81

own before we moved to Florida and had to give him up. He starts purring, with his tail up. Now, there is an old-fashioned picnic basket sitting off to one side. I open the top and take out some piping hot chicken, French fries, mashed potatoes, and stuffing.

The plates are all white with gold around the rims. The same with the glasses and of course the utensils are gold as well. I'm finishing the last piece of chicken when who walks up, but my grandfather and grandmother! I jump up and give them big hugs as tears run down my cheeks.

"I've missed you so very much from the first day you were gone." I give them bear hugs at the same time. They were both young looking and seemed to be in their late twenties. I asked, "What have you been doing since you got here?"

"Well," said my grandmother. "We have just been enjoying heaven. There are always new people to meet here; places to go."

"If I had known you were going to be here I would have saved you some chicken."

"It's nice to see you," they said, "but we have to be going now. We will see you again soon." I give them a big bear hug again, then they just walk away, waving good-bye. Tears are running down my cheeks. I'm sorry to see them go.

The Lord gets up saying, "Don't worry, my son, soon you will be here forever and you can see them any time you want." With that thought in mind, we exchange our good-bye hugs.

Swimming Hole

The Lord is saying, "Come here," in a nice way. I am in glory again in the twinkling of an eye. I wish things were that fast on Earth, sometimes it feels like the 1800s. It's night time on Earth, but in heaven everything is so bright. Now I find myself at one of the many swimming holes.

I'm standing watching all the children playing. I look around for the Lord because I just arrived, but I don't see him anywhere. I have swimming trunks on in the twinkle of an eye, I just have to think it. I run for the water as fast as I can. Bam! I hit the water with a big splash. Everyone looks to see who made such a big splash!

The water is clear and refreshing. I take a gulp; one doesn't have to worry that the water will get dirty from everyone swimming in it. I'm guessing the water in the middle is about 10 feet deep. There is also a big slide at one end of the swimming hole. It doesn't just go straight into the water! It goes every which way, up, down, sideways and then straight.

I make a mad dash towards it, excited as I make my way up the steps. At the top I raise my hands, "Hurray," I yell as I start to go down. The slide is smooth and slippery. It's made of a plastic kind of shell-like substance; *you know how sometimes they crush shells together in order to make something else, well that's the way the slide is.*

Going over the bump I find myself airborne. Man, this is so awesome! I hit the water with a big splash. Some of it goes up my nose because of the force of the water. I don't see any sign of the Lord but I still go on. I look out to see the Lord as I come out of the water again.

He is standing on the grass just watching me. I climb out of the water and run up to him. "Come on, let's go together!" I'm pulling his arm as I say it.

He says with a smile, "Well . . . I suppose I could go down once, I guess!" No sooner has He said that than he is dressed in swimming trunks. Now we are now both running towards the slide. *Just try to let your mind go for a moment will you. I know it will be hard for some of the religious people, ha, ha, but just try for a second. Just picture in your mind me and the Lord running together with a pair of swim trunks on towards a swimming hole!* The Lord gets there first; He goes up and waits for me to come up behind him.

I get into position putting both of my arms around him. He shouts, "Are you ready? Here we go!" We both push off going over the bump at the same time. We are traveling super-fast! The Lord smacks the water first; I follow a split second after, I give the Lord a high five. We have to get out of the way quickly because more kids are coming down the slide.

Suddenly, it dawns on me that I have never seen anyone carrying towels when they swim in heaven, so I ask the Lord about it.

He laughs. "Remember, in heaven you just have to think of things and they happen!"

"Yes, Lord."

He continues, "Well it's like that. No one wants to dry themselves when they get out of the water, so it is automatic."

"I understand Lord, I had so much fun."

"Yes, so did I. You have to be going now."

"Alright," I respond. Now, I'm home.

The Lord's House

as I sit in my bedroom at my wife's computer, the Lord says, "Come on up. I'm ready." *I guess I have to be ready at a moment's notice.* This time I'm standing on top of one of the walls in heaven. The Lord appears, cupping his hands around his mouth to make sure I hear him, "How are you, my son?"

"Where did you come from? I didn't see you anywhere when I landed on top of this wall," I inquire as I jump down.

The Lord is dressed in a light yellow shirt with black dress pants and black shoes. Just then I have a strawberry rhubarb pie in my hand. It is the best tasting pie, ever! Oh, can't forget the milk! *It may seem that I talk about eating a lot; well, I talk about every one of my experiences just to show you what heaven is really like.*

I notice we are walking into a park setting. I see birds, grass, trees, and flowers just like you see down on Earth. Up ahead I see a large group of buildings that look to be made of gold. The Lord says, "Come my son, I want to show you my home."

I thought heaven was your home. He reads my thoughts and says, "My son, heaven is where my house is, also the capital of my kingdom."

As we walk toward his house there are two ponds, one on each side of the grassy hill. They are filled with goldfish and lily pads, just like the ones at the front gates. As I get closer I hear the blast of trumpets in unison. The Lord looks at me saying, "They are proclaiming my arrival!" You can tell it's the Lord's home because it seems to shine brighter than all the other buildings.

It has a bunch of stairs leading up to the main doors. We walk up to the front doors. There are two of them, each made of wood with gold handles. They are quite heavy, and I had to open one door with both hands. The first thing I notice is the white marble floor. Then, I notice the living room off to the right side. He says, "Come my son." He has two chairs with a matching couch that is made up of the softest of leather that hugs every inch of our new bodies.

As I'm enjoying the chair, I notice on the wall Leonardo da Vinci's painting, the Mona Lisa! "Does Leonardo know you?"

He smiles, "Yes my son, he does. He painted this for me."

I am at a loss for words. "Lord, I had no idea that you were a connoisseur of fine art."

"Oh yes, who do you think gave Leonardo his artistic talents?"

The dining room is huge. The table is made up of the same wood as the front doors. Next, we enter the kitchen. It seems normal; sink, kitchen cupboards, even his dishes. I see a stove off to one side. Pointing to it I ask, "What do you need that for?

"My son, sometimes I just like doing things the old-fashioned way."

Now, we turn a corner and go up a flight of stairs. He has three bedrooms. I go into the main bedroom, it has a double bed, with a bright red bed spread. I ask, "Lord, why on earth do you need a bed?"

"It just feels good, doesn't it?" I reply, "Yes Lord, you're right."

He continues, "Just like your bathtub in your tree house."

"Yeah, Lord," I reply, getting the point.

He has a dresser beside the bed. I nod in it's direction and ask, "May I?"

"Sure."

So, I go over and open the first drawer. It has all kinds of shirts, neatly folded. I then walk over to the clothes hutch with double doors that match the front doors. I pull open both doors at once. I see a number of robes neatly folded on the top shelf in different colors. On the second shelf he has pants stacked five high in rows and on the bottom shelf is a row of dress shoes.

Next, I go out on the balcony which has a railing all around it. I look down and see a swimming pool. At one end there is a Lion's head with water coming out of its mouth.

"Lord, may I go take a swim?"

"Sure."

I run down the stairs, not even looking to see what is in the other two bedrooms. Immediately, I jump in, making a huge splash. The Lord just stands there laughing. I climb out and jump in again and swim to the other end. Wow, what a rush!

The Lord walks up to me as I come out of the pool saying, "My son, you really have to be going." I give him a hug; now I'm back home.

Dodo Bird

All is quiet on the western front; the wife is in bed. While I was in the shower earlier today I was asking the Lord about my father, and how he's doing spiritually? The Lord replied at this point he is just waiting to die, which made me very sad. He also said that He was working on him, but if he died tonight he might very well end up in hell.

The Lord asked me a while ago not to pray for him or my stepmother because I would ruin the work He has already done on him. I know we like to pray for loved ones, but sometimes you have to take your hands off so to speak, and just let the Lord do his thing.

"Enter through the narrow gate. For wide is the gate and broad is the road that leads to destruction, and many may enter it. But small is the gate and narrow the road that leads to life, and only few find it" (Matthew 7:13-14).

The Lord died for everyone, but not everyone is going to make it to heaven. I hear the Lord calling me now and find myself floating across one of the walls to heaven! *When you're in the spirit you can do anything.* The Lord is there, standing and looking at me with both hands on his hips. I ask, "Lord, how did I do?"

"Pretty well, for a part timer. Come on, I'll be your tour guide for a little while."

In front of us is a stream with a white oval bridge over it. The water is moving in the opposite direction than what we would see on Earth. All I have time to do is say, "Lord," before He answers, "The water is going towards the throne room." I bent down to take a sip.

In the distance I see a cherry tree in full bloom. I run up for a closer look. Wow, what a wonderful smell. I'm looking for any blossoms that may have fallen on the ground, but that would mean that something had died in heaven, which is not possible. The Lord says to me, "My son, it always stays in bloom 24/7."

We walk through a very fancy garden. It has a golden walkway that is about four feet wide. Nothing in heaven is fake; if it looks like gold it is gold. I'm looking at both sides of the walkway and see snapdragons and tulips. There is a bench off to one side, so I take a short break in order to take it all in. As I'm sitting there, a huge dragonfly lands on my hand. I look into his big eyes and see many different colors.

Now the Lord says, "Come my son, I want to show you something." I follow him a couple of steps and then see a skinny bird, something like a Northern Loon but with a smaller neck. This one looks vaguely familiar. I remember see-ing it in pictures. The Lord scoops it up in his hands and says it is a Dodo bird! My mouth drops open and I stare at it in shock.

"Wow Lord, they killed the Dodo during the 17th century."

"It's a shame that man had to wipe out one of my creations from off of earth completely!" As He was talking I was petting the bird's head. It stood about two feet high and had skinny legs and a slim build. *All the pictures and books that I have ever seen portray the Dodo as being short, fat, and unable to fly very far.*

90

The Lord tells me my time is up. "I'll see you soon, okay?" I reply sadly, "Yes, Lord."

I have since done some research on my own and this is what I have discovered about the Dodo bird. It really is thin like I saw in heaven. Look at the article "The Dodo bird: An example of survival of the fittest," published in September 1995 by Jerry Bergman.

Angel's Dressing Room

The Lord says, "Come on." So, now I'm in heaven. I run up to the Lord and give him a big hug. He puts his arm around me saying, "So, how are you really, my son?"

"I'm glad to be here Lord, but I have to admit I'm not looking forward to going to work tomorrow." *I'm just saying what's on my heart since He knows it anyways.*

"Yes my son, I know, but soon you will be released from it."

"How soon?" I ask.

"Let's just say very soon; you have learned almost everything that you need to know." I bowed down before him in humility, saying, thank you Lord, over-and-over again.

"Now arise, my son," He says as He touches my shoulder. I get up with tears in my eyes. Next the Lord says to me, "Come here, I want to show you something." He puts his hand on my shoulder again and immediately we are standing in front of a building with a lot of windows. We walk inside and hear whispers saying, "The Lord is here." My eyes have to get used to the difference in glory for a second.

I see angels being fitted for their clothing. It's just like a tailor shop, with one angel having an assistant measuring how tall the angels are etc. to ensure the royal robes fit, for the ones that go before the Lord in the throne room. Some of the angels are standing around talking to one another, waiting to be measured. They are wearing loincloths while waiting. Some talk about different places on Earth they've been to, others are just talking about the Lord; just making small talk.

Now, the Lord says to me, "I have to go now, you can come back later to see what's going on."

The next day the Lord meets me just outside the same building. We go inside and the first thing I see is the glory cloud. I thought they didn't have glory clouds in heaven, just on Earth. To help you envision what a glory cloud looks like, picture going into a smoke-filled room.

While that is what a glory cloud looks like, the Glory of the Lord is present all around. I guess with all these angels going in and out of the Lord's presence all the time is why I see it now. I ask the Lord, "Do they have more than one robe to wear?"

He laughs, "Of course they do." We walk over to a chair where there is a white robe with gold piping around the edges.

"Lord," I ask, "if we can just think of clothes and bam, they are on us, why do they do it the old-fashioned way?"

He explains, "Because they just like doing it, plus they all like getting together to have a good time."

I answer, "Oh yeah, that makes sense. Lord, can I be fitted with a robe?"

Sure, He says. "Stand over here while one of the angels takes your measurements."

I'm asked what kind of material I would like to wear. "Hmm, let's see; how about a white silk one with lots of gold piping on it," pointing to the one on the chair. "Oh, and a red one too!"

The angel says, "You can have whatever colors you like."

Now, the Lord comes over to me saying "My son, your time is up."

"Oh Lord, just a little while longer, please!" To my surprise He agrees.

"Where would you like to go?"

"How about a park, I really like them."

"Okay," He says as we are sitting on a park bench. I can hear the crickets singing and it's not even dark yet. *Not that it gets dark in heaven, but that's when one would normally hear them.*

The Lord taps my shoulder gently. "My son, it really is time for you to go."

"Oh, okay."

Mermaids

I saw a television show on mermaids once, which got me thinking and asking myself did the Lord create mermaids? Perhaps there is more to it than simply a drunken sailor's imagination. I did some research on the subject and this is what I found.

On January 4, 1493, Christopher Columbus actually saw mermaids. He was no drunken sailor; he was a highly respected man of his time. On June 15, 1608, Henry Hudson also saw a mermaid. He said, "She was looking earnestly at my men, she had very white skin, long black hair, with a tail like a porpoise." He was the man who started the Hudson Bay Company in Canada. Like Columbus, he was a very well-respected man during his era.

Now I hear the Lord asking, "Are you coming, my son?"

"I'm ready Lord." Instantly, I find myself in heaven. It's so beautiful and peaceful here. *It's nice to get away from Earth, even if just for a little while. Just like when I used to visit my father's cottage. It was about 200 miles away from the city, near a lake. It was so nice to visit and get away from it all.*

The Lord greets me near a park setting wearing dark pants and a white shirt. "How are you doing?" He asks.

"I'm fine Lord." He puts his arm around my shoulder.

As we start walking He says, "I see you're writing about my mermaids, my son." I have created them and they are highly intellectual beings."

"Lord," I asked, "Why did you make them look like men and women, yet have the tail of a porpoise? Doesn't it degrade man?"

He looks at me, "On the contrary my son, I think so highly of man that I copied his bodily form. I take pleasure in watching them swim around and play. Unlike man, they don't have a soul, just a spirit. I liken them to the four winged angels that are in my throne room." He continues, "Do you remember the movie *Splash*, with Tom Hanks?"

"Yeah, I've watched that movie a hundred times."

"Well, let's just say that parts of that movie are not far from the truth."

I can't contain myself anymore. "Lord, do you have mermaids in heaven?"

"I have many."

"Lord, I have never seen any whenever I've been swimming."

"You were not ready my son, but now you are ready! Let's go see my mermaids."

Now, I'm getting really excited. The Lord takes me to a high waterfall. I don't

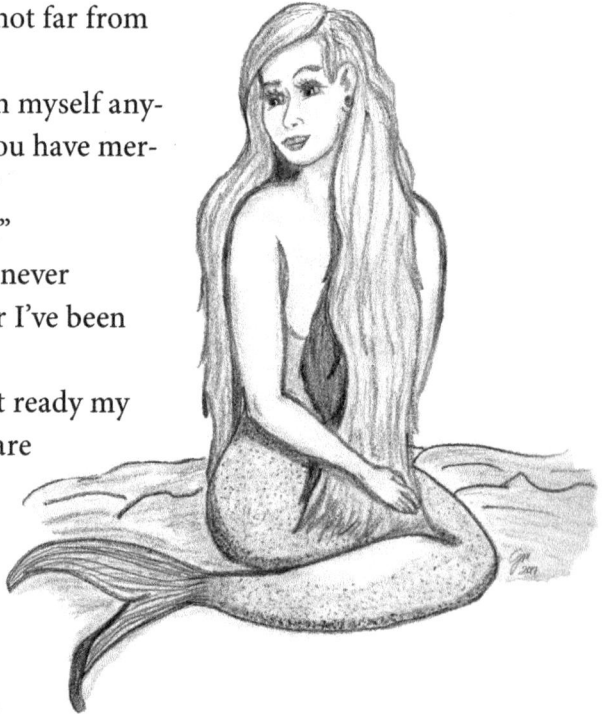

think I have ever been to this one before. It has crystal clear water and children are playing nearby. I see some adults too. We have to talk a little bit louder to each other, because of the thunder from the water that is crashing down below.

I am at the bottom of the falls. I slide into the choppy water. The Lord wades in behind me and now we are in the middle of the drop off where the water collects from the falls. I look down, and to my amazement I see my first mermaid! She beautiful! She has long, dirty blonde hair, a round face and blue eyes. Her tail starts just below her waist. I ask the Lord If I can meet her. He says, "Sure," laughing. He touches the water with the palm of his hand. She surfaces and swims over.

Her tail has webbing between the two larger parts. The whole tail section is a light blue. It seems to change between light blue to a darker blue depending on how the light hits it.

"Lord," I exclaimed. "Oh I wish she had a soul."

"Yes my son, I know. But, only humans have souls."

"But Lord, you could put one in!"

"Yes I could have, but I said, 'Let us make man in our image.' Not the creatures of the sea."

"What does she eat?"

"A lot of plants, crabs, mussels, that kind of thing."
Now, the Lord says, "You have to go now, my son. I'll see you later." We hug.

The Lord Talks about Hell

The Lord is good all the time. Although I'm currently between jobs, I'm still in the center of his will. While I am eating lunch, I ask the Lord, what about people in hell. The reason for the question is I had gone on YouTube and was watching people who claim to have gone to hell and back. I ask the Lord, "Don't you hear the cries coming from hell?"

He answers, "I do hear them, but they had their chance. No one in hell has to be there."

"Everyone has made their own personal choice to follow me or not! My word says, 'For since the creation of the world God's invisible qualities, his eternal power and divine nature have been clearly seen, being understood from what has been made, so that men are without excuse'" (Romans 1:20).

The Lord continues, "Hell was created for the devil and the fallen angels that listened to him and tried to overthrow my kingdom. The hearts of the people who go to hell are the same as the Devil's; so, I don't have any choice but to place them there. People often say, 'How could a loving god send people to hell?' I don't. You send yourself."

Now I'm in the presence of Jesus himself. We are sitting at a table. The Lord says, "I want to talk about something with you." He starts by saying "My son, I'm like an earthly father, slow to anger, quick to forgive; although I chasten my children when they get out of hand." I look at him. "But mostly you're a loving father, right?"

He responds, "Yes my son, my mercy endures forever and so does my love."

"In life you only get one shot. The punishment for sin is hell. You have your entire life to repent; it only takes twenty seconds. Just like the jailer who was in charge of the prison where Paul and Silas were imprisoned. He asked, 'What must I do in order to be saved?' That was it! How many seconds did that take?"

We give each other a high five.

"My son, I try not to think of the souls in hell. That's one of the reasons why I go for walks through my kingdom to celebrate life."

"Come, my son. I'm glad we had this chat," He says as He strokes my hair.

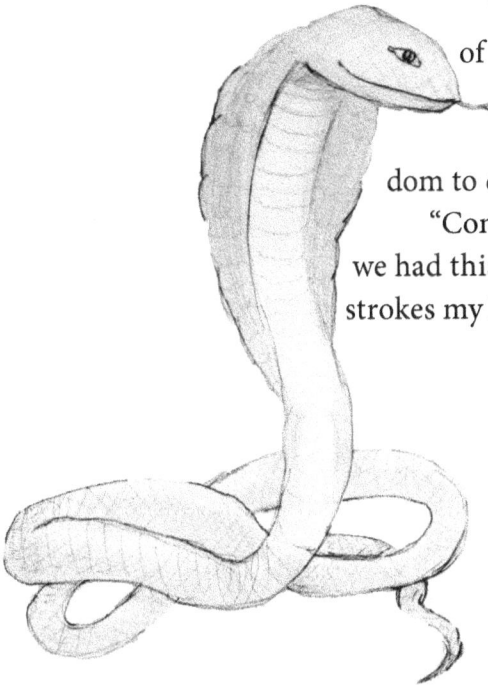

Bottled Water

I'm in the bedroom, needing a change from being in my living room. It really doesn't matter where I start, it's where I finish that matters. "Come on, my son. I'm waiting for your arrival."

Okay Lord, I answer.

I hear the Lord again, "Are you coming?"

"Yeah Lord, just one second!" I find myself sitting on the bottom tier of the singing fountain.

The Lord walks up to me. "How are you doing, my son?"

"I'm fine," I reply. I feel that I have been away for so long. I take a sip of water from the fountain and boy it tastes so good. There is nothing like that on Earth! "You know, Lord, if I could only bottle this water from heaven I could call it 'heavenly water.'"

He laughed, "Yes, my son, that sounds like a great idea, except for one thing! How would you get the water from heaven to Earth?"

"Well Lord, that's where you come in, since you made water come out of the rock in the desert, I was thinking you could have water from heaven come out of the ground!"

"Hmm, I see." Suddenly, I notice a strong-smelling fragrance filling my nostrils. It seems to come in waves. "That smell is coming from me my son. It's the Lily of the Valley."

"Wow Lord, it's beautiful. How many fragrances do you have?"

"Many, my son. You see, I'm always creating and this includes fragrances."

The Lord tells me to have a seat and we both sit down on what seems to be white metal chairs. The Lord says the only metal in heaven is gold. I ask him how it is that the chairs are white; are they painted? He tells me they are not, so I bend down to look at them more closely. Now they look transparent. I can see right through them. "Lord, you planned this."

"Nothing is by chance, my son. You wanted to learn something new, and I know you are very inquisitive." I can see the Lord is really enjoying this.

"On Earth you call it white gold, but this is real white gold. Now, He informs me that's it's time for me to go so we hug and now I'm back.

Father

Right now, I'm at the gates of heaven, just watching people walk in and out. Yes, just by thinking about heaven I arrive. Now, I see the Lord walking up to me "How are you doing, my son?"

"I'm fine, Lord."

"What's on your mind, my son?" *As if He didn't know already!*

"Why don't you show me around anymore?"

"Well, there are parts of heaven you can't see, because you're only part time. My son, there is so much for you to learn here in heaven. Where do you want to go?"

He rarely asks me this unless I'm being set up. Let me think, hmm. "Can I go see your Father?"

He looks me in the eyes with a piercing stare. "Are you sure you want to see him?"

"Yes," I reply, "I'm sure."

We are now just walking along, saying "Hi" to everyone who passes us.

The Lord stops. "Well, my son, let's go the fast way." We arrive at the steps leading to the Father's place. It's a building that sits off by itself with many steps leading up to the main doors. As we proceed to climb the stairs I nudge the Lord. "I'm going to take the elevator, okay?" He just looks at me and laughs.

Boy, I didn't think Christmas would come so early! Remember I said He laughs just like Santa Claus. We get to the top, open the double doors, and then turn right down a hallway. We then turn left and go down a short hallway. At the end of this hallway I see The Father sitting in a huge room. All I hear is "Holy, Holy, Holy." As we get closer, all of a sudden my knees start to feel wobbly.

The Lord grabs me just in time to prevent me from falling. I see a mist-like substance in the air all around. This must be his glory cloud. As I enter, I see angels standing five rows deep and about thirty to a row. These are just the ones behind his throne! I sense all of the angels watching me, probably because I don't have any robes on! I see the four winged angels standing at the Father's throne as described in Revelation. I feel my lungs breathing in his glory which is so thick you could cut it with a knife!

I see a rainbow encircling one section of the roof. It's not flat but round and high. There are two sets of pillars standing about 10 feet apart and going up to the first section of the round roof. I also see angels singing with street clothes on. Now I find myself singing and clapping. I just can't help myself. This goes on for what seems about an hour or so. *Since there is no time here this is just an educated guess.*

I'm standing about 10 feet away from the actual throne itself. All I can see of the father is a bit of his face and beard and some white hair. I also see part of his feet and on his left hand a signet ring is on his pinky finger. The Father motions me to come closer. I don't know if I can. I might fall over because of the Glory! I hear him with my mind, He doesn't move his lips. I don't see them anyway.

He motions me to come even closer! I gingerly move about five steps closer, so now I'm about a foot away from him! My knees are starting to feel like Jell-O®! I'm glad the Lord is standing right behind me. He asks, "How are you my son?"

"I'm fine Father, and you?"

"I'm fine also."

"Thank you for taking the time to see me."

He smiles saying, "You're very welcome. Is anything on your mind?"

I say, "No," shaking my head. "I just wanted to meet you and say Hi." He nods his head in response. I say goodbye, Father. He smiles as if knowing. I turn to the Lord, "I have to go to bed, this experience has really drained my strength."

The Lord smiles, "I'll see you later." We hug and now I'm back.

Milky Way

I asked the Lord earlier in the day if it was possible to come visit him sometime soon. He let me know that today was a good day. I am caught up into heaven just by thinking about it. *He told me that I can come and go as I please, but He still tells me when my time is up.*

The Lord is sitting on a park bench in the middle of a park, of course. He gets up as soon as He sees me and gives me a big hug. "How are you doing, my son? Are you doing okay?"

"Yes, I'm doing fine." I exclaim, "Lord, you look particularly happy."

"Well, my son, the church is getting ready for my return. With my help I'm moving them right along. Things are getting darker, my son. Be ready, when you see things start to appear don't be alarmed, but instead know they must come to pass.

"Where would you like to go?"

"I know!" I jumped up as if I were still in school and had the answer before anybody else. "The Milky Way!"

"Okay, grab my hand." No sooner have I grabbed his hand than we are there, near the center of the Milky Way! Wow, what a sight. The stars that seemed so small to the naked eye are so big now.

I also see more colors as I looked deep inside the Milky Way as we move deeper into the center. *As I have probably told you, one can breathe underwater in heaven. Likewise, one does not need a space suit or oxygen in space because you're in your spiritual body.* I'm in the middle of the Milky Way, just hovering you might say. Me and the Lord; wow what a rush!

I see a lot of blue color, so I ask the Lord about it. He says, "It's because of the vast number of stars that make up this particular cluster of stars that you call the Milky Way. I get much pleasure in the works of my hands."

"Lord, do you ever visit any of the other galaxies in your vast universe?"

"Oh yes, my son, all the time. They may be millions or billions of light years away, but time and distance is nothing for me."

'Lord, how many stars make up the Milky Way?"

He laughs. "Several hundred billion, my son, and I know them all by name."

I take another hard look at the outside of the Milky Way; we are in the middle of it. I see more colors like blue, red, white, and yellow. "Lord," I ask, "are there really different colors like I seem to see?"

"Yes, my son. The colors of stars are determined by the temperatures and compositions of their outer layers. Thus, they may be many colors plus many wavelengths your eyes cannot see.

One planet seems to stand out more than the others. It has a blue hue around it. I point it out to the Lord. He says, "Yes, I like that one too. It's many light years away."

Still looking at it, I ask, "What's it like?"

He says, "Much like Earth."

All I can say is, "Really?"

"Yes, my son, there are many planets in different solar systems that are just like Earth."

"Lord, do they have life as we know it?"

He looked at me again. "Yes, my son, but I only died for the souls on planet Earth because they rebelled against my perfect will. Out of all that I have created it was the only one where I made man in my own image."

"And we are the only ones that have Holy Spirit living inside of us, and you sent him to Earth to help us out, right?"

"Yes my son, you are spot on."

"Now my son, we have to be going." We hug in the middle of the Milky Way; now I'm back.

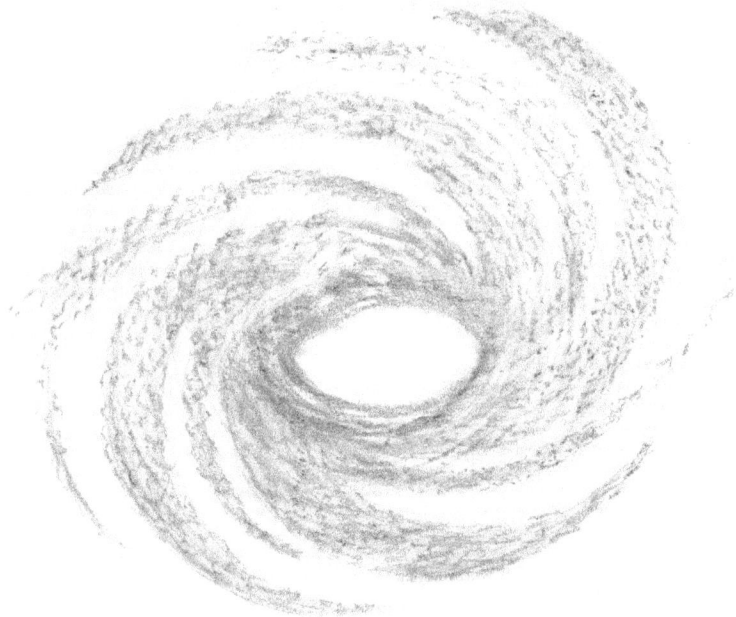

Foolish Virgins

I'm sitting in my bedroom, minding my own business when the Lord shows up, sitting on my bed! He says, "I have a couple of things on my mind that I want you to write down for me."

I quickly reply, "Sure."

He starts by saying, "Halloween is coming soon, my son. I am not looking forward to the ritual. Men's minds have been blinded by the enemy."

"Small innocent children have been drawn into it by their mothers and fathers. It reminds me of when Moses came down from the mountaintop, and the Israelites were doing all sorts of evil deeds. This is what Halloween reminds me of. My anger burns as the day gets closer and the world makes preparation for it. At times, I have to turn away because of the stench that fills my nostrils.

"My own people ask 'How have we turned away to other gods?' when they are indulging in the very act of adultery themselves! One of the biggest lies the Devil uses in the churches today is to dress their young people up in so-called friendly costumes, imitating people from my word. These churches are not led by my Holy Spirit. They are just like the

Israelites going up to the high places to worship other gods. This is exactly what they are doing!

"Just like the ten virgins, five had enough oil while five ran out! Congregations are filled to overflowing as they sing empty praises to me. My eyes run to and fro, looking for the true people to set apart. The watchmen have fallen asleep. They have failed to warn the people in these last days. They have refused to acknowledge my Holy Spirit and walk in my ways. They have refused to humble themselves before me. I classify them as foolish virgins."

Then the Lord says, "This is what is heavy on my heart. Please, tell my people." I quickly get up off of my chair, give him a hug and He disappeared as fast as He appeared.

Christmas

Well, it's Dec. 24th and all through my house not a creature is stirring, not even a mouse. I snuggle down under my covers with visions of sugar plums dancing in my head. Tonight, my wife and I went out to a candlelight Christmas service. About the three wise men, I hate to burst anybody's bubbles but they were Magi, they didn't see the Lord until two years after his birth, when they brought him gifts.

Now, I'm at the front gates. The Lord puts me where He wants me in heaven. He greets me with "Hi, my son," shaking my hand. "I have a surprise for you."

"Really!?" My eyes widen. I know when He has a surprise it's really fantastic. He hands me a package. It's not very big, probably 2 x 2-inches with bright red paper and a red bow. It's a shame to rip off the paper. I open the lid and it's a diamond ring. It's gorgeous! The center stone an emerald and is flawless. It is surrounded by smaller diamonds—exquisite.

I put it on my ring finger and the sparkle almost blinds me! He tells me to read the inscription inside the band. It says, "To Richard, at Christmas." I give him a big hug. "Thank you so very much, Lord."

He smiles and says, "You're very welcome. I knew you would love it."

"Lord, where are all these people going?" I stop a girl who has dark, smooth skin and ask her, "How are you?"

"Fine."

"What's your name?"

"Virginia."

"How old are you?"

"Twenty-one."

Oh really? I look intently at her. She looks like she is thirteen.

"So, how long have you been here?"

"Oh, about a hundred years, your time."

I was taken aback by how long she had been here. She looked so fresh, like she just arrived yesterday. I guess when I've been here 100 years I'll still look the same as I do now. I asked what she did all day and if she got bored.

"Oh no, right now I'm helping organize a marriage supper and making sure everything runs smoothly."

I asked if maybe we could go bike riding sometime. She replies with a smile that would lighten up any room, "Why yes, I would like that very much." Then off she goes.

"Lord," I say, "I miss the snow, but not the cold."

He laughs, "Yes my son, I know what you mean. Well, you can go to the mountains and go skiing."

"Really?" I exclaim with excitement. Now I'm at the top of a hill covered in fluffy snow and guess what, it's not cold! Most people are just wearing sweaters or t-shirts. I have a pair of nice looking red skis. I turn around, looking for the Lord but he's nowhere to be found.

Just then an angel is standing beside me with an iron armband on the upper portion of his forearm, indicating he's a member of the Lord's elite fighting army. He shakes my hand,

"Hi, my name is Tom and I'll be your escort. The Lord has some unfinished business He has to take care of. Don't let my looks fool you, I'm quite harmless to the saints."

I really don't feel like skiing so I decide to just walk around. Now I'm instantly transported down to where the shops are.

I walk into a coffee shop where they are serving hot chocolate and ask for a cup. As I am being served, I notice Tom entering the shop. I turn to him and say, "I still have to get used to being served something and not paying for it."

He smiles, "Is that so!"

As we turn to leave he asks, "Would you like to hold my shield for a moment?"

"Sure." He carefully hands me his shield. It's too heavy for me and falls to the ground with a big thud! He just looks at me.

"I'm sorry. I didn't realize it was so heavy!"

He laughs. "It's quite okay, Rich." He picks it up as if it were a feather.

Tom ask, "Are you finished looking at everything?"

"No," I said, but now I realize why he asked me this question. It's probably time for me to go.

I turn to him and just as I'm about to ask he says, "Yes Rich; it's time for you to go." I shake his hand and now I'm back.

Grandma's Place

There was a cold wind blowing,
as I walked up the steps to Grandma's place.
This winter was one of the coldest I could remember.
Grandma must have seen me coming;
she opened the door and gave me a big hug.
The smell of sugar cookies filled my nostrils
as I begin to thaw out.
I wonder if she made them
for old Saint Nick.

Grandma must be getting really old,
she has looked the same ever since I can remember.
I asked her, "What did you do before you were Grandma?"
She smiled, "I looked after you.
Your mother had to work.
Grandpa pitched in when he was in the mood.
Now, young one, go wash your hands,
we have a lot of work to do."

The kitchen was smothered
in the heavy aroma of Christmas turkey.
My mouth watered with anticipation.

She had a big dish of cranberry sauce.
The meal wouldn't be complete
without Grandma's secret recipes.

She tells me they were handed down
from her grandmother.
Christmas wouldn't be the same
without her famous Pumpkin Pie.

A warm glow filled the room
as the fire crackled and popped.
I felt a gentle warmth against my face.
I struggled to stay awake, and of course,
in Grandpa's favorite sleeping chair.

I wish I could stay
at Grandma's place for good.
I have ever so fond memories.
Her gentle voice and kind words
match perfectly with the Christmas season.

It just would not be the same
without visiting Grandma's place.

Fighting the Enemy for Real

I know," says the Lord, "that you have had a very rough day spiritually." I see Him motioning me to come to his kingdom. Instantly, I'm here in heaven. The great thing is that I don't need a plane ticket or reservation to get here.

I meet the Lord at the singing fountain where He puts his arm around me saying, "My son, remember a while ago when I took you to where the angels were making swords?"

"Yeah," I say, and He continues.

"Well, I want you to go there and see Michael my archangel, he's expecting you."

Where the angels make their swords is something like a blacksmith shop. They make them the old-fashioned way by heating the metal and then pounding it into shape. Now I'm walking to the building where I was before. I open the door and each angel stops what they are doing look at me, *not in a bad way*. Out of the midst of them comes a very muscular angel.

He puts out his hand saying, "Hi my name is Michael." I am at a complete loss for words again and just say, "Wow, I have finally gotten to meet you!" He just smiles and says, "And you are Richard the Lion Hearted! Come with me," as he puts his arm around me. We start walking past the other angels who are all working on their swords.

"I have a sword for you," he says.

"You what?!"

"You heard me right. I have a sword for you."

He then hands me a golden sheath with a slight curve. I take the sword out. The metal is astounding. It's a glistening bright metal that almost blinds you as the light reflects off of it, like a Samurai sword.

"The Lord and I know you like Samurai swords so we had one especially fashioned just for you."

It has a dark blue grip and in the middle is a dark blue stone. Despite the power and strength emanating from the blade it is as light as a feather. Yet, a close look at the edge reveals it is sharper than a surgeons' scalpel. I ask if I can use it. "Funny you should ask, seeing as we are going out to do battle right now. You can come along."

The entire company of angels assembles outside the building. They are lined up in perfect formation. The group is called to attention, all the heels clicking together sounds like the crack of a rifle. Addressing the group, Michael says, "We will be traveling to one of the many portals between heaven and Earth. Some of the enemy's troops are there; we have to nullify them."

I really don't quite know what he means by "nullify" because spirits don't die. Then look- ing at me he says, "We have

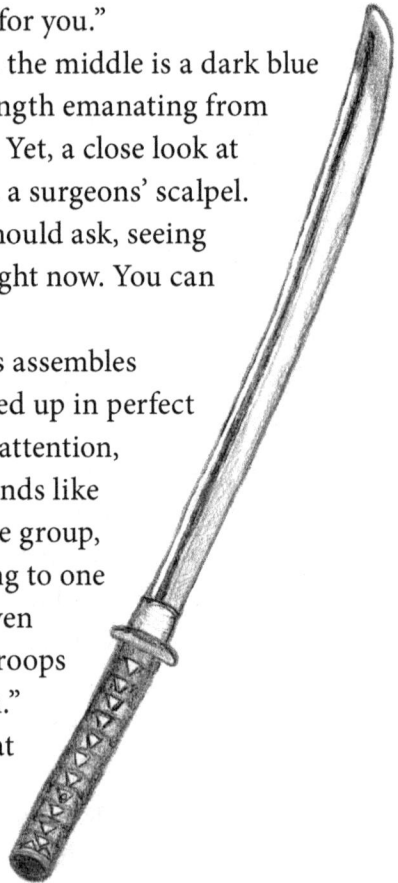

everything you will need," then he hands me a red sleeveless robe that goes down to my ankles and tells me to put it on. Next, he gives me a round shield with a cross embossed on the front. Unlike my sword, the shield is very heavy, about 30 pounds, and looks like dirty brass that has aged.

I put my right arm through the straps in back of it. He then hands me my sword and asks. "Are you ready?"

I answer heartily, "Lets rock and roll!"

As we near the portal I notice the enemy also has swords and shields. However, unlike ours which are in pristine condition, theirs appeared old and deformed. Some of them are black while others are dirty brown. Most of them have black wings for the crest. Suddenly I find myself standing in mid-air, with angels on both sides of me.

The enemy appears to notice that I am not an angel and mistakenly assumes I am an easy target! I ready my sword to meet them. I raise my shield to block a blow to my head from one of the demons. He has dark red eyes recessed deeply into his head. He then tries for my side, but I block that too! Now it's my turn. I make a move with my sword towards his head. My offensive move appears to catch him off guard. I suspect he was assuming I would be scared and confine my moves to protecting myself. The sword glances off his temple, striking his shoulder. He cries out in pain. Hmm, I think they don't die but that's how you push them back. Plus they don't bleed.

Michael comes over to me saying, "Good job Richard the Lion Hearted." The rest of the troop took care of the enemy in short order. "So, what do you think?"

"It was very exciting pushing the enemy back."

"Well, we'll have to take you out again then won't we?"

I reply, "Of course." Then he said it was time for me to go and now I'm back home.

I want to share with you something that happened to me a day before I typed this chapter. I was surfing the internet while sitting at my deck near the front window of our house. It was about eight in the morning when all of a sudden I saw a shadow that I assumed to be a person. You can always tell if someone is looking inside your house from the outside. It was overcast which made the shadow even darker. I rushed to the front door to see what was going on, but when I opened the door there wasn't anyone there! I looked both ways and saw no one. Only a few seconds had passed from the time I saw the shadow and if it were a person there is no way they could have disappeared so quickly.

Then the Lord let me know what had really taken place. The figure I saw wasn't human. It was a spiritual being that had taken on a human form. It was one of the enemy's workers keeping tabs on me, trying to scare me into not writing this chapter. All I saw was it was wearing a dark black robe. I could only see the back of its hands and feet. It stood about five feet tall and had a thin build. This was the first time I had seen a member of the spiritual world manifest itself in the physical world.

The word of God tells us to beware, because the enemy walks around like a roaring lion, seeking victims to devour. (1 Peter 5:8)

In the Movies

Now the Lord is calling me. I have made an appointment with him so I don't want to miss it. Almost like a doctor's appointment, where some places charge you a fee if you miss it. I'm glad the Lord doesn't charge for seeing him! Now I'm on the main drag; a lot of people are dancing and I hear music. The Lord walks up and gives me the normal greetings. I just put my arms around him and give him a big bear hug. He looks at me and asks, "What was that for?"

"I just wanted to show my love for you Lord."

"What would you like to do my son?"

"Well, could we go to the movie theater? I want to be in an actual movie with the 'Duke', John Wayne." No sooner have the words left my mouth than we are at the movie theater. I think everything in heaven has two big doors at the front, and the movie theater is no exception.

The theater is a fairly big building, but from the outside there is nothing that would attract your attention. In fact, it is rather plain looking. As I go in I am struck by how, unlike down here on Earth, the lobby with its drinks and popcorn is not dimly lit. The lobby area features four large pillars made of gold placed in each corner. The only thing missing is the pricing of the drinks and snacks. Inside the actual theater, the floor on the main section has a gradual slant towards the screen. Down towards the front on each side of the screen is a pair of staircases leading up to the balcony.

The carpet is dark red and the seats are an off-red not quite as dark as the carpet. The seats are to die for, very soft and comfy. The walls contain paintings of either flowers or a countryside setting in large fancy frames. The ceiling features chandeliers that are beautiful but not large or gaudy. Immediately in front of the screen is a wooden stage about four feet high and twelve feet across, running from wall to wall. On each side is a pair of small steps leading up to the stage. Like movie theaters from years past, a curtain is in front of the stage.

Once the curtains open up a large screen descends from the roof. As I walk on stage a broad-shouldered man walks up to me. He shakes my hand and says, "You must be Richard."

"Quite so. You must be John Wayne!"

"You got that right, partner."

"You know, my favorite movie was *True Grit*."

"Is that so?" he said in true John Wayne fashion. "Well guess what. We are showing *True Grit* right now as a matter of fact! After about five minutes I want you to just step inside of the picture, just like Mary Poppins."

"Okay," then went and sat down, so people wouldn't be looking at me instead of the movie. At the five-minute mark I

walked up to the screen and put one foot up to it. Then I push the screen, with the heal of my foot; it just disappears. So, I decide to just go for it and step all the way into the screen.

Wow! I find myself right in the movie during the wild west of the 1800s. John walks up to me, hands me a Winchester repeating rifle, and asks, "You do know how to use one of these don't you?"

"Oh yes."

"Good." Then he gives me a handful of cartridges and motions for me to run behind a big rock. He follows saying, "I want you to open fire on the fellows who will be coming down the trail anytime now. They are the bad guys okay, so you don't need to worry about shooting first then asking questions later." I just nod my head and do what I'm told.

There is no director, lights or anything like you would see if this was filming a movie. I'm actually in the 1800s. After a few minutes, I hear the bad guys coming up around the corner. Keeping under cover, I take aim then squeeze off about five rounds, killing one of the bad guys. I yell to John, "I got one of them!" He comes over to me, "Good shooting!" *I don't think they are really dead, because in the making of the movie they would be stunt men.*

This is the first time I am at the movies in heaven.

The second time the Lord and I have very good seats, which is the very middle center row. It's a huge screen showing Captain Nemo in *20,000 Leagues Under the Sea*. I have popcorn and a drink, so does the Lord. I find myself saying out loud "I wish I could be in the movie." I casually take some of his popcorn.

Lord, I ask, "Could I go into the movie?"

"Yes, sure. Go stand by the screen, pick the scene you want, and just walk in!" I casually walk up on stage and wait until the scene with the giant squid on the outside of the submarine during a storm begins. I just step in.

I find myself on the outside of the sub; harpoon in hand; waiting for the right timing to throw. I get my chance then in it goes right next to the giant beak. The wind is so violent that I have to attach a lifeline to prevent being washed overboard. Also, I have to duck the large tentacles with its dangerous suction cups.

Finally, the squid slips beneath the waves; I go below deck with everyone else. They treat me like one of the crew. Walking up to the front of the sub, Captain Nemo puts his hand on my shoulder and says to me, "Good job." He smiles, "Thank you." I look out the huge glass, watching the divers with the old-fashioned diving suits gather supper for the crew.

I know this is hard for some of you to grasp, but this is the way it is here in heaven. Now I hear the Lord saying it's time for me to go. I'm thrust out of the picture and back into my bedroom.

Butterflies

I'm just relaxing next to my computer when I hear in the spirit "Man, are you ready?"

"Ready for what?" I know very well it's the Lord; I'm just messing with him. He has a good sense of humor once you get to know him. As I'm writing this down I just happened to look out my window and a huge butterfly passes by. *My wife has a green thumb so we have a lot of flowers and plants that attract them.*

It's not as big as the ones in heaven though. I hear the Lord again, "Come on! I'm waiting!" He didn't mean it in a bad way.

Now, I'm walking on the main drag, just looking at the gold that makes up the streets, admiring all the different colors reflected in the gold. As I walk the Lord meets me. The first question I ask is "Lord, do you have a place where the butterflies are? You know, a place where you keep them all?"

He looks at me saying, "Funny you should mention this. As a matter of fact we do have such a place!"

I can hardly stand still, I am so excited. "Lord, why didn't you show me this earlier, like years ago?" He put his hand on his chin as if in deep thought. "Well my son, most probably you were not ready to see the reality of it; plus I had other things to show you instead." Now we are in front of a grayish building with what seems to be a big glass dome in the middle.

We proceed to the front doors which are made up of very expensive wood with gold handles. As we walk in right away I notice the marble floors. They are off-white with gold and brown colors running through the stone. As I continue walking I notice a series of rooms around the perimeter opposite of where the dome is. Each room has glass enclosures each with a cocoon at various stages of development.

"Lord," I ask, "do butterflies ever get hungry?"

"No my son, they just drink nectar like you will see later on saucers at various places throughout this building. I would expect the climate of this butterfly oasis to be very humid, but the air is dry just like the rest of heaven. Now, the Lord says to me, "Have a look around my son." The first place I go is the dome. Underneath it's like a miniature forest with tropical plants and it contains every imaginable flower. There's a water-fall in the middle on the floor with goldfish swimming around. They are not as big as the ones in the duck pond though.

I'm taken aback by all the beauty. I have to sit down to take it all in. As I do, a butterfly lands on my hand. It's yellow and black with a black body and a wing span of about 16

inches. It just sits there for a moment before flying away. No sooner has it left than another butterfly lands on my shoulder. This one is dark blue, about the same size. It sits there for about five minutes before it too goes on its way.

I'm just sitting there enjoying the waterfall, looking at the goldfish when all of a sudden an even bigger butterfly lands on my knee. This one is about 20 inches with gold wings! Yes, gold wings. They actually look like bright gold; I just don't know any other way to explain it.

Oh yes, I almost forgot; on top of the water at the bottom of the waterfall are lily pads with big frogs on top of them. These frogs are not the normal green color with a lighter side underneath. These frogs are different colors. Some are very dark blue with green eyes, some are yellow with black spots on top; some are even red, just like they had been imported from the Amazon.

Now, the Lord turns to me saying, "Well, my son." I know what's coming next; He hears my thoughts again saying, "Yes my son, it's time for you to go. Isn't this place beautiful?"

"Yeah Lord, its breathtaking!" He then tells me that He comes here often just to sit and relax, looking at his creation. And now I am back.

The Other Side of Heaven

When people think of heaven they think of it as one big place, and it is; but since I'm not living there and only visit, I am only allowed to go to certain places. This is why I call this chapter the other side of heaven. I'm home when I am in heaven and Earth feels like I'm on vacation. I really can't stand this vacation any longer; I so want to go home.

The Lord greets me at the fountain. He smiles and shakes my hand as I ask him right off the bat, "Lord, can I see what's over there?" pointing to buildings that I have only seen at a distance.

"Come on, let's go then, but remember there are places you're not permitted to go because you're only part time." So, we start walking south of the fountain when all of a sudden we are walking in a very nice neighborhood.

I think we walked a couple of blocks. I see really nice houses. I'd say if they were on Earth they would cost about $300,000. Most have stone fronts, not brick like on Earth. Some have flowers on the side; others have fountains in the front. There are no sidewalks, no garages, no street lights, or sewers. You get the picture.

Children are playing in front of the houses. *I want to say streets but there are no roads for cars.* Some are flying kites, boys are running with their dogs while others are riding bikes. Some people are just walking around. "Come on," He says.

I see another neighborhood in the distance, with tall buildings just beyond that. "Lord, may I ask what is in those buildings?"

"Oh my son, various things are going on but mostly you can't see inside, although you can look outside.

Now we are near a forest. The Lord asks if I would like to see what the forest is like. I reply that I would, so we continue further. We are moving in and out around trees with thick foliage. This forest is teaming with life; small colorful frogs, walking sticks, and snakes. The first one I see is a light brown snake. I run over and pick it up. It's about six feet long. I yell to the Lord who is just ahead of me "Look Lord." He turns around, watching me put the snake around my neck. "I can wear it as a large necklace." He just laughs. *Remember that unlike the animals on Earth the ones in heaven are very docile.* That reminds me, once I had to learn this fact the hard way. I was at my tree house; there was a big pond behind it with an alligator. The Lord had asked me to go up to it and start stroking its head. Naturally I said, "Yeah right."

But, He insisted. I thought it would just rip off my arm and go into a death roll! But, if you know the Lord and He insists, you know He has the best intentions. So, I

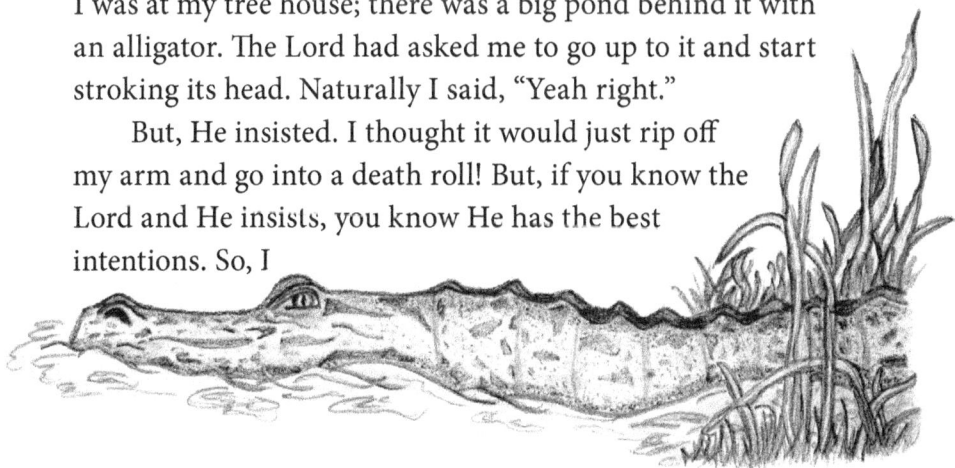

start to go up to the alligator, saying out loud "Here boy, good boy," sweat dripping off my head. *Your new body doesn't sweat but you get the picture.* As if I could appease the alligator by saying these things. I started inching toward him, but he's not moving. I'm thinking he's sizing me up and figuring out how many mouthfuls it would take to finish me off.

Once I'm standing next to the alligator the Lord says to me "Don't be shy, just start petting his head. He likes it." Umm hmm, so I gingerly put out my hand to stroke his head. I'm thinking all the while what it would be like to have one arm. I start stroking his head and notice that his skin is very rough, that's probably why he likes it. I stroke him about ten times, by now the Lord is laughing so hard I think He's going to faint!

I turn to him saying, "What?"

After He composes himself somewhat He said, "You see, he really liked it. Every animal in heaven that I have created is docile. They will not harm you in any way, they don't even think the way animals do on earth; it's not in their nature. Sin hasn't corrupted them. This was my experience of that aspect of heaven.

As we continue walking I hear the distinct sound of waterfalls. The sight is breathtaking. The sound becomes deafening. When we are about 20 feet from the base of the falls I turn to the Lord asking if we can go swimming. No sooner did I say than I have a pair of dark blue swim trunks on. The Lord has a pair of red ones on. He says, "I thought you would never ask." We both laugh. Are you ready He says, grabbing my hand.

I'm thinking oh no, were going to jump! "On three," He says. I nod. "Three!" and down we go. It only takes a few seconds before we hit with a big splash. Wow that was fantastic! Just then a dolphin surfaces. The Lord grabs onto its fluke and under He goes. He's down for about five minutes then surfaces. I'm just swimming on my back, waiting for him. We swim to the shore then He says to me, "Well, have you enjoyed your-self, my son?"

"Lord, no words can explain the joy I have had with you!" We hug, now I'm back.

Visit to Mars

I find myself at the front gates of heaven. As usual, I try to play music by brushing up against some of the rungs a certain way. I think it sounds pretty good. By now the Lord is standing nearby, watching me do my thing! I ask him what He thinks. "Well, my son, I think you could use a drum set with it."

I ask the Lord, "You know the planet Mars? Well, I have never been there."

"Let's go." He grabs my hand and we take off just like a jet; up, up and away.

As I look behind me heaven is suddenly getting really tiny. We are headed for a planet that looks brownish red in color. Now we start moving into Mars' atmosphere. *As you know, in the spirit you don't need a space suit or anything.* Now, we touch down on the surface. Wow, its really barren here. All I can see is a lot of rocks and gradual hills along with a lot of sand.

"Lord," I inquire, "why do you have a planet where nothing grows?" He says, "My son, I get pleasure from Mars just being in existence. My ways are beyond your ways." I shrug my shoulders, take hold of his hand and we're off. Heaven is quickly coming into view. We land at the singing fountain and I take a drink of water.

I have been looking at time travel on YouTube and it got me to wondering, so I go to the best source I know. "Lord, is there really such a thing as time travel? I heard they perfected it in the 1940s and are still using it today."

He puts his arm around me, saying as we walk away from the fountain, "My son, it is true that they have created a way to travel through time. I gave man this wisdom to use it for the betterment of mankind, and what do they do? They used it for their own selfish purposes."

"In a way, you engage in time travel when you come to heaven. You instantly travel though space and time."

"Yeah Lord," I exclaim. So why is the government keeping it a secret?"

"Well my son, if they admit to time travel they must also admit to the higher power who created it in the first place. They can't have that now can they? And yes, there are people living on Mars right now; they have been there for a long time now."

"Lord, I didn't see any houses or man-made structures while we were there!"

"No my son, they are on the other side of Mars, living beneath the surface.

They don't want any of this to come out and get to the masses because eventually the evidence would point to a creator, which is me; but they want to take all the credit for these things."

"So why is man on Mars anyways?"

"Because it gives them a sense of achievement. They look at themselves saying 'Look at what we have done.'"

Billy the Kid

I hear the Lord say, "I'm waiting."

I reply, "Okay, hold on." Now, I'm at the fountain in heaven. The Lord comes up to me and gives me a big hug. I recently watched a movie about Billy the Kid. Afterwards I checked out his story on the internet. So, I ask the Lord about him. He says to me "Yes my son, Billy was a murderer. He killed many people in his day, but sadly he didn't have to kill anyone."

"I still love him, but he is still waiting in hell for his trial. Would you like to go and see him?" Oh man, I wasn't planning on going to hell tonight; it is not in my plans. Hmm, I think to myself; I haven't been to hell in a long time. He smiles at me saying, "You're right."

"Okay, I'll go! But don't leave my side, okay Lord?"

"Yes my son, I will be right beside you."

No sooner has He said this than I am transported high above the earth. Looking down, I see what seemed to be funnels, like tornadoes. The Lord says, "These funnels are actually pathways to hell. We are going to take one."

Instantly, we start moving towards one. Just before we entered the eye I can hear a loud swirling sound. Suddenly, we are in the middle of it, going down, down, down. As we are descending I notice it getting hotter and hotter. The stench that comes along with it smells like rotten, burning flesh.

Suddenly, we stop descending and find ourselves in the middle of a huge cavern. I can hear the cries of the dammed! They cry out because they remember all of the chances they had to accept the Lord while on earth that they didn't take it. Instead, they chose to believe the lie the Devil always tells people; "You have plenty of time to accept the Lord. Just go ahead and take care of it tomorrow." The problem is for the vast majority of people tomorrow never comes.

As my eyes adjust to the semi-darkness I can see individual cells with black bars lined up, dug into the cavern walls. The cells are longer than they were wide; I'd say they are about 10 x 20 feet. They are all joined together side-by-side. Above each cell is a plaque with a date. It lists their date of death. The Lord says, "Let's take a walk over here," so we move closer to the rows of cells. The first cell we come to says, "Billy the Kid, 1881."

I look inside and there he is, standing about 5 feet 3 inches tall, but just a skeleton. He looks up as if glad to see us saying, "Lord, can you let me out now? I have learned my lesson. I'm sorry for killing all those people. I even heard the gospel in the small gold mining town I lived in, but I didn't want anything to do with it. I just wanted to have fun. Killing people gave notoriety and made me feel important."

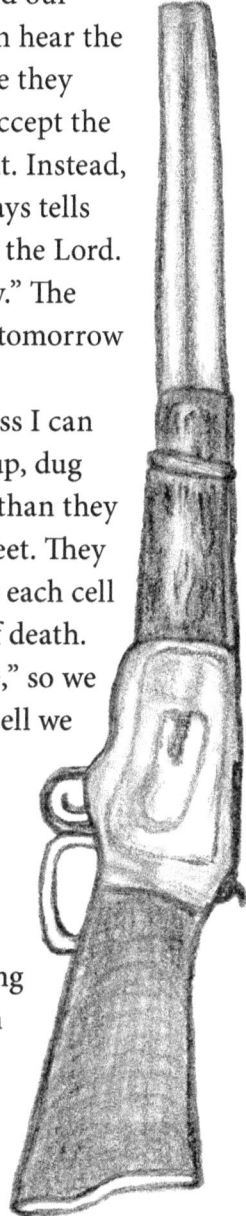

The Lord answered, "It isn't about this life; it's what comes after the physical that's important."

"Lord, after I went to jail the first time I should have learned my lesson and looked for an honest way of life."

My heart was broken over what I was hearing; I blurted out, "Lord I feel so sorry for him, isn't there anything you can do?"

"No my son, I have done everything I can do! I died for his sins, but he didn't take the straight and narrow road. Instead he chose the broad way that leads to destruction."

"You see, Billy had plenty of chances to give himself up, take his punishment and repent of his sins. They still would have hanged him, but at least he would be with me in my kingdom!" The Lord put his hand on my shoulder. "Time for you to go home, my son." We hug and say goodbye, now I'm back.

Skipping

I am waiting patiently for the Lord; trying to keep my mind focused on him, not letting the things that went on today hinder my mind. Now, I'm standing at the front gates. You see in heaven you don't think upon the day's events, hoping for the next day to be better. There are no days in heaven, just one big long day. Every moment in heaven is better than any day you have ever experienced on Earth. I give the Lord a big hug, I didn't wait for him to initiate it this time.

The Lord starts by saying, "You're at the end of your 'Desert Storm', my son!"

Some of you may be experiencing desert situations in your life, but I'm here to tell you to hang in there baby, you'll make it! The Lord isn't finished with you yet. If I can, you can also.

I turn to the Lord's and give him a high five.

I ask the Lord if I can go skip-a-rope. He looks at me and says, "Sure you can." *Some of you might never have heard of skip-a-rope! It's done by taking two ropes going every which way, and one has to skip over them, trying not to get tripped up. That is the best way to explain it.* I don't have to wait long before I see two girls with ropes. I run up to them, introduce myself, and ask if I can play with them?

They giggled and say, "Sure," with red faces. I guess they are shy, quiet girls, about 10 or 11 years old. I ask them their names. One is named Sandy and the other is Agatha. Sandy has red hair; I love red hair. Agatha has black hair and is wearing a jump suit with a white shirt underneath with checkers on it. Sandy has on a green dress, white socks, and black shoes. *I thought I would tell you a bit about them since they now have a part in this book.*

Another interesting thing I notice is that as I look at the skipping rope I has gold strands mixed in. So, at a distance the rope looks like it's made of pure gold. Agatha asks, "We haven't seen you around, did you just get here?"

"No, I come here for visits."

"Oh, you must be Rich!"

Now, I find my face turning beet red. "Well yes, that's me. Why? Do I have a reputation?"

"Oh yes, we hear about you all the time! We just have never met you in person that's all."

"Do I have a good reputation?"

They both laugh. "We wanted to meet you; you're kind of cute."

I don't know what to say. I blurt out, "You can read my mind?"

They look at each other and say, "Yes we can!" in perfect unison.

"I thought only the Lord could read minds."

"Nope," Sandy says. "We all have bodies like the Lord, so we can read minds just like He can." Now, they've got my curiosity up, so I ask them how long they have been here.

"Fifty years ago we were best friends," Sandy said pointing to Agatha. We were in a car and my father was taking us to the store. We took a curve too fast and it caused the car to roll over a cliff; both of us were killed right away. The Lord sent angels to come and get us the moment we died.

My father was okay, he was just shaken up. Eventually he got over the grief of us both being killed. We prayed that he would make it to heaven too, but he wanted to do the worldly stuff. Unfortunately, he died without knowing the Lord personally and the dark angels came for him when he died.

All I could do was say, "I'm sorry he didn't make it, but you prayed for him."

"Yes," Agatha said, "just because you pray for someone doesn't mean they will make it. We all have a free will and it's up to every individual to make up their own minds."

In order to lighten the conversation I said, "Okay, let's play twosies; *meaning grabbing the rope at each end on both sides, making it swing both ways.* I take the rope; Sandy had the other end and Agatha was in the middle. Boy she's doing really well, not missing a beat. She motions me to come in while she takes over my spot with the rope. I jump the first onslaught of rope before I get in the rhythm. Okay, now I'm on my hands and feet at the same time. If you could see me now!

Out of the corner of my eye, as I stand up I see a girl talking to Sandy. She wants to jump in with me. Sandy makes the hand gesture and I reply, "Okay." Now, the new girl is jumping with me in perfect unison. The Lord walks up to us, making the same hand gesture. He wants in so the other girl jumps out, making room for the Lord. The Lord waits for the opening then he's in! We are skipping together; wow, what a moment! Then we both bow out together. He says, "That was fun!"

"Yeah, we'll have to do it more often." We both laugh.

He looks at me with all the love in his eyes and says, "Your time is up, my son. You have to be going."

I say good-bye to the girls and give each one of them a hug. I say to them, "I look forward to seeing you two again." The Lord then sends me home.

Girl Friends

'm sitting here all alone, waiting for the Lord during my quiet time. All of a sudden, He says, "I'm waiting for you, my son." Now, I find myself in glory with him! I am walking down the main drag of heaven, admiring the streets of gold. This time is different; I see a blue hue in the gold. I ask the Lord about it and He says, "My son, everything changes when you get here. The laws of physics no longer apply here in heaven."

I ask, "Does the gold change to any other colors?"

He laughs, "Of course they do! Red, light green, brown, and every color of the rainbow!"

We are about two blocks from the front gates when the Lord says, "My son, I want to talk to you." Putting his arm around my shoulder, we start walking back the other way. He starts by saying, "I know it's hard for you to be unemployed. I have done a good work inside of you that you're not aware of my son."

"I am opening the doors to employment for you to be blessed." *I did find a job for a while. It lasted four months; they paid me the most I had ever earned. You see, the Lord might be trying to accomplish something inside of you but sometimes the only way He can do these things is by taking drastic measures.*

As I stand there He hands me my bike. *Didn't I tell you that He had given me a bike? It's all red and a cross between a mountain bike and a road bike, but it goes really fast. I have gone up and down hills and valleys with it. I even raced it with other people. Once on my way down the main drag I passed someone riding a similar bike that was lime green I just blew past him.* After getting back from my bike ride the Lord asks if I enjoyed it. I tell him, "Oh yes, very much."

I notice a lot of very pretty girls here that look my age. I just have never mentioned them before. He lifts up his eyebrows looking at me. I continue "You say there's no marriage in heaven, but can I still go out on a date with them?"

He answers, "No my son, there is no marriage in heaven so why would you need to date since isn't that the purpose of dating; to find a life partner and then get married?"

"Yeah Lord I understand, but can I still look?"

"Of course you can look at the beauty I have created. You can even ask them to eat with you or have an ice cream cone; but they would just think you're a nice guy, that's all!

They think differently than you do. You will see this for yourself when you're full-time. Now He says, "Well my son, it's time for you to go."

"But Lord, I just got here. I mean, I'm having the time of my life and I don't want to leave!" He puts his hand on my shoulder again saying, "I know my son, but you'll be coming back real soon." We hug; now I'm back home.

His Wounds

I t's getting late, Lord."

"I know, my son, do you want to come right now?"

"Yes." Walking down the main drag I have a ring on the middle finger of my right hand. It's made of heavy gold and has a dark green emerald in the middle. *If you want to see it you will have to meet me one day.* I just thought it and it appeared.

The Lord meets me next to the main gates. He says, "Follow me." We go off the main drag into a grassy section. He unbuttons his shirt then drops it to the ground. He turns to me saying, "I want to show you something to enable you to tell people what I went through for them as you describe what you see."

He turns around with his back facing me then says softly, "Look and touch my son!"

I start touching his scars. The ones on his back are deeper than I had imagined. They are pinkish in color, not smooth as one would think but jagged. I put my finger in them ask Him if they hurt. He says, "No, not after two thousand years."

The skin is a bit tighter than the other parts and isn't as elasticized as the rest of the skin. The scars on his back go every which way, even across his shoulders, and then over to the upper part of his chest. His neck had some scars on them too. Now, He turns sideways to let me see the wound where the Roman soldier pierced his side.

It looks like it started at the sixth rib then went up at an angle. I felt it, and it was jagged like the tissue on his back. It looks like it went in more and seemed to be about three to four inches across. Now, He turns back facing me. He picks up his shirt and puts out both hands, so I could see the scars on his wrist. Then, He removes his sandals to let me see the scars on both of his feet.

He says to me ,"It's one thing to describe what I went through, but it's quite another to let someone see the actual results. I gently put my hand on his wrists to feel where the nails went through them. I think they are about three quarters of an inch in diameter across and one eight of an inch deep. Then I kneel down to feel the wounds on his feet.

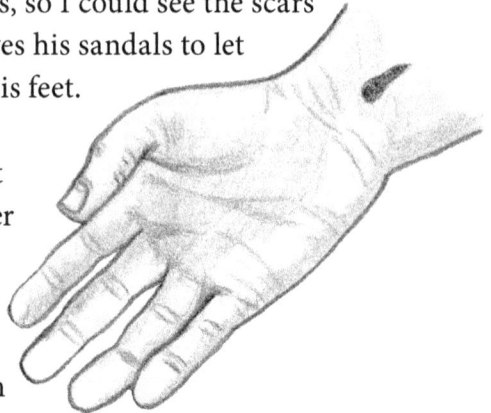

They are at the top of each foot. "Man, that must have been unbearable agony, Lord," I exclaimed with tears welling up in my eyes! *When you consider all of the little bones that make up the foot even attempting to stand up would have involved unspeakable pain.*

The Lord just looks at me and says, "I could have erased all this from my body when I rose from the dead, but I wanted to remind people for all the ages what I have done for all of mankind."

I continued to feel the holes in his feet; they both looked the same size. He then puts his sandals back on. I just gave him a hug, that's all I could do at this point.

Now, on to a lighter side of things; the Lord says to me, "I want you to meet someone that you'll be happy to meet." I looked up the street and here comes King David wearing a crown. He comes closer saying, "Oh you must be Richard. I have heard only good things about you." I shake his hand saying, "Hi, King David." *I'll try to describe him the best I can.*

He stands about 5 feet 2 inches tall, stocky built, muscular arms, red hair, and a beard which is not quite as bright of a red as his hair. He's wearing a crown of gold on his head. I can't stop staring at it. *I'm a jeweler by trade, so that's why I'm so interested in his gold crown!* I ask if I can take a look at his crown. He takes a quick glance at the Lord who nods his approval and then proceeds to hand it to me. It weighs about five pounds and is encrusted with precious stones all around.

"Can I try it on?" is my next question. He nods in the affirmative. Wow, it fits really nice; it's just the right size! My head size is about ten. I take a few steps in it and notice it could get heavy very fast while walking around. I hand him back his crown and he puts it back on his head again. I ask, "David, do you wear your crown often?"

"No, just once in a while; whenever I feel like it."

"Oh."

"Well, it's been nice meeting you Richard; till next time. Good bye." Then, he turns and walks away.

I look at the Lord. "Well, that was really short, how come?"

He laughed, "He's not much of a talker sometimes, but he observes a lot."

Choir

It's late at night. I've just arrived home from church, and now I hear the Lord saying, "I'm waiting, my son."

"Lord," I respond, "I'm a bit tired but I'll try and make it."

"I'm waiting!"

"Okay," and once again I find myself in the presence of the Lord. Man, it seems like it's been forever since I last saw him.

I was sick in the body all week, which made it seem extra-long. The Lord walks up to me and politely asks, "How are you doing, my son," as He shakes my hand.

"I'm fine Lord, just glad to be home."

He smiles, "Well my son, where and what would you like to do?"

I reply, "What? You don't have anything planned for me?"

He shakes his head no.

I'm at a loss for words. "Well Lord, after thinking about your offer, I think I'll just join one of your fine music groups."

He raised his eyebrows saying, "You will huh? I guess you could then."

I think to myself this is a little strange because every other time his response is, "Sure you can." But, this time it is different. I ask him about his response and He tells me, "Oh, it's just that I don't know if you'll fit in, but just try to do your best, okay?"

"Sure Lord," then instantly we are in front of a huge building.

I didn't have a clue about what is inside, you know the Lord is always full of surprises. I see many angels, about a hundred or so, outside just talking. I can't help but wonder how many are inside. The front doors consist of magnificent stained glass of every color imaginable. Most of the angels are dressed in white robes, while some are in street clothes; however almost every one of them is wearing sandals.

I try, in vain, to listen to their conversations but can't make anything out. It's just like trying to listen to people talking far away where you know they are speaking but can't hear the individual words. Suddenly, they start filing in. I watch for a couple of seconds then quietly enter with them.

Immediately upon entering, I notice a greeting area in the front before you walk into a huge arena with a stage in front. It reminds me of a movie theater. As the angels take their places, I noticed none of them are sitting down. After about an hour the whole place is packed.

All I can see is a solid field of white. Suddenly, the choir director comes out with a baton in his hand. When he raises his hands the whole place erupts into a joyous chorus of songs of praise. As the angels are singing my eyes are drawn to the center of the stage. It looks like lights are coming from the air just above the director's head in all different colors. I'm awestruck at what I'm seeing. I immediately look for the light fixtures, but don't see any.

As I'm taking all this in the Lord says to me, "My son, you will understand fully when your full time comes. Now it's time for you to go. You have been here quite some time now." So, we say good-bye to each other; now I'm home.

Chariot Ride

I have set some time aside for you, my son," the Lord said as He spoke to my spirit man. Now I'm on the main drag. I love looking at all the different colors in the golden streets. The Lord looks down at my feet to see what I'm looking at.

"Lord," I exclaim, "I am just admiring all the colors in your streets of gold."

"Oh I see," He replies while waving his hand in front of me. Instantly, instead of the main drag I see all the different colors start to become crystal clear! I mean, I can see right through it. I'm actually looking out into space right now.

The Lord starts to laugh just like Santa again.

"What's so funny," I ask.

"Oh, just the look on your face," He says as he waves his hand. I give a little chuckle myself. Now, He asks me, "Where would you like to go?"

"Well, I am happy just to be here at home with you. But, since you asked, I would like to go on a chariot ride."

He laughs. "You would now, would you?"

"Yeah Lord," I'm still looking at him.

"Okay then, let's go." The next thing I know I'm between two big gold chariots that look like the ones in the movie

Ben-Hur, going around in the Circus Maximus where the chariot races in ancient Rome were held.

There are some differences, though. These are made of solid gold and stand about eight feet high. They have six gold handles on the inside, three on each side with scrolls embedded in them. The wheels look like old-fashioned stagecoach wheels. However, these spokes are not made of wood; instead they are a lighter color of gold and attached to an even lighter colored hub.

A white horse stands in front with golden reins. The Lord says, "Up you go, all aboard."

I stand up to grab one of the handles on the inside. *We are just going to go at a good pace, take a couple of turns and that will be it.* NOT! The Lord gets in beside me, asking if I am okay.

"Yeah," I reply, not knowing what to expect.

The Lord shouts, "Let's go!"

We start out slowly, which is a good thing. Then we begin to pick up speed. At this point I can hear the wind in my ears.

Now, we begin to pick up more speed, and then we begin to gradually lift off the ground. Up and up we go, above the tree tops before finally leveling off. I really don't know how fast we are going, but the ground beneath us is zipping by pretty quickly. All of a sudden, the Lord yells out "Turn left," then bam we make a hard left. I'd say we go about another mile before the Lord yells out, "Turn right, then take us home."

We make a hard right then start to descend. The next thing I know we are back where we started. I jump out with the Lord right behind me. He asks, "Well, how did you like that, my son?"

"Wow Lord, that was awesome!"

"Yes, now you have to be going home." I just shrug my shoulders and give him a big hug. Now I'm back home.

Hugging Angels

Well, I messed up last night. I 'fell asleep at the wheel' so to speak. I wanted to spend some quiet time with the Lord. But, this is a new day. I will rejoice and be glad in it. Now, the Lord is saying, "Come on. I've been expecting you, my son."

I find myself standing on the main drag once again. I run up to the Lord and give him a big hug. "Wow Lord, I really missed you! I'm sorry I haven't come sooner, but this new job . . . my body has just been aching all over so I don't feel my best."

He folds his arms saying, "My son, this job of yours is just temporary. I have sent you there to talk to certain individuals and then you'll be moving on. I know you really hate this job, but be of good cheer, my son. Soon you will be out of there."

Just then one of his angels comes up to us. The Lord gives him a big hug, asking, "So how did it go?"

The angel replies, "It went as well as planned. Everything is fine."

The Lord said, "Good," and the angel left. That's the first time I have seen any angel hug the Lord, so I just had to ask, "Lord, why did that angel hug you?"

The Lord laughs, "My son, angels have emotions just like you do. They may not be human, but each one has their own personality. They like to be hugged too!" *Hmmm, I never thought about that before.*

"So, what was the conversation about, Lord?"

He smiles, "Oh, just heavenly business. That's all you need to know; run of the mill stuff. No biggie." I just shrug my shoulders. It is clear the Lord doesn't want to elaborate, so He lets me down gently without hurting my feelings.

I look around and everything seems to be the same, when all of a sudden another angel comes up to us and the Lord asks me, "Why don't you give him a hug!"

He is about six feet tall with wings, all dressed in white. I walk up to throw out my arms around him; as I get closer, I just put my arms around his whole body, wings and all. He says, "That was really sweet; I enjoyed your hug, Richard." I just smiled. I'm still getting used to the notion that angels have feelings and aren't just robots.

The Lord says to me, "My son, remember, angels are just like the redeemed, except they don't have a soul because they are in their permanent state, not like my Church waiting for their glorified body. Here, he hands me a hot fudge sundae."

Wow, is this really good; especially the syrup! I motion to the Lord to see if He wants a bite, and to my surprise, He says yes! Instantly He has a gold spoon in his hand. The handle has the Coat of Arms on it, just like his father's signet ring.

He dips into the ice cream. "Mmm, this is really good." *Can you wrap your head around what just happened? The Lord of the Universe letting me have ice cream with him! I'm going to remember this moment for a very long time.* Now, the Lord says to me, "Your time is up, my son."

"Really? I haven't gone anywhere yet!" He puts his hand on my shoulder, "I know, but just wait till next time, okay?"

"Yeah" is all I can say. Now, I'm back home.

Apple Trees

Feeling lonely for the Lord, I ask if I can spend some much-needed time with him. Of course, He said yes. Now I'm here, not waiting for him to say, "Come on." I find myself walking in a big field, my tree house is visible in the distance. So, naturally I start walking towards it, when all of a sudden the Lord appears beside me.

I let out a gasp, taken a bit aback because someone just appeared next to me, when a split second before there was no one there! "Why do you do that?"

"Do what?"

"Appear from somewhere else just like that," I respond as I snap my fingers. He raises his hands saying, "My son, what I do is perfectly normal up here. Everyone does it sooner or later. Remember, all one has to do is just think of things and they appear."

The Lord asks if I want to go to my tree house. I tell him I don't feel like it anymore. "Okay, where do you want to go?"

"Lord, can I come back tomorrow. I'm really tired from the day, please?"

He puts his arm around me and says, "Okay." I arrive back home.

The next day I am in my room sitting alone, just pondering on the Lord when I hear with my spiritual ears, "I'm waiting for you my son."

Bam! Just that fast I find myself in the presence of the Lord. I find myself walking towards an apple tree. Usually when I am by trees in heaven, they are oak trees. I find myself in a park setting. This tree was all by itself. As I walk up to the tree, the Lord has not shown up yet. I notice some apples are red, but most of them are green.

As I am standing there looking at the tree, suddenly Lord is standing beside me. He asks, "My son, do you know what those green apples represent?"

I respond, "I assume they are a picture of the people sitting in churches who have been there for quite some time, but are only getting a little nourishment from the services, which represent the branches they are on, but they never grow to maturity."

"And the red ones?"

"Well, these are the people who hear the word and let it sink in to maturity. Thus, they are full of goodness and love." He then picks a red one and bites into it saying, "You're exactly right my son. You listened to your heart and didn't let your eyes dictate to you."

"My son, you can't do anything about the green ones. For just like in the natural realm, they sit in one place, moving every once in a while when the wind blows, taking in very little nourishment from the branch, thus in the spiritual, they only move when someone excites them. They sit in church, stuck in their own ways of thought, not wanting to grow any further, only changing their thinking slightly. As a result, they never grow to spiritual maturity. Just like in the natural, they will always remain green. I will take care of these apples, but I will give them little thought."

"Lord," I exclaim, excited by what He has just told me. "Did you teach like that when you where on earth?"

"Yes," He said with a twinkle in his eyes. "I take a green apple and bite into it; lo and behold, I got one with a worm in it!"

"Oh yes, my son," he's finishing his train of thought. "The worm represents the inside of the people, who have unforgiveness in their heart, holding resentment towards other Christians. You see, all that remains of that green apple you just bit into." I look at the inside; it is almost all gone. He continues, "That's the inside of these people spiritually, there's nothing left. As you see, the apple is mostly hollow on the inside, but still green on the outside, thus appearing to be growing to maturity. As we both know, there is no decay in heaven. I just wanted to bring home my point."

"If you don't forgive someone of what they did to you, your heavenly father won't forgive you. I said this in Matthew 6:14–15." So, I take a bite of a red one and it was very juicy and delicious. The Lord then lets me know that my time is fading away and it is time to go back home. We hug and now I'm back.

Camouflaged

Here it's almost Christmas; another year closer to the Lord's returning. I really miss Christmas when it's over. When all the houses are lit up with all the festive lights, people really seem happier this time of year. Being in Florida we don't get snow. I miss the white stuff. But, I do not miss the cold! The Lord is saying, as usual, "Come on, I'm waiting." Now, I am in his presence.

I find myself standing at the entrance to a forest with the walls of heaven off in the distance. I see the Lord walking towards me wearing a camouflage jacket with matching pants. Instead of saying hi, my mouth just falls to the ground. I exclaim, "Lord why are you wearing those!?" He says, "I just felt like wearing these to see you since we are in a forest environment."

"I'm not going hunting; I just wear them for relaxation. *I know this is going to blow your mind when you read this, because many of you still think people walk around in robes all the time in heaven.*" I walk up to him and notice his clothes are crisply pressed, smelling brand new, like Lavender. He laughs, asking if I want a set. I reply, "Yes, but they have to be exactly like yours." Bam! Just that fast I have a set of camouflage clothes exactly like the ones the Lord has on. I really wasn't expecting to wear them at that moment. They also smell like lavender.

The Lord holds out his hand, "Come with me." He takes me by the hand and we walk about a mile before coming to a big pond. The pond isn't huge, but it's not small either. It has lily pads with huge bullfrogs on top of them. *As I looked closer, I can see that they aren't like the ones on Earth, but then again most everything here is different than on Earth.*

Some have green eyes, some blue, while others have orange eyes. The most amazing things is that their body colors matched their eyes. But, not all are like that! Some have different colored eyes— different from the body colors. For example, if a frog had an orange colored body their eyes might be a light or dark blue.

Some of their eyes resembled cat's eyes, but to my disappointment, none had camouflaged colors. I looked at the Lord in amazement. "Lord, how come you never showed this to me before?" He laughs, "You would have rejected it before! Heaven has many treasures."

I have to sit down to try and get a grip on all of this. I ask the Lord if they are friendly. He laughs, reminding me that everything here is docile. I stretch out my hand to the bullfrog closest to me, then all of a sudden it jumps onto the bank next to me and stares at me with its big green eyes. I gently pick it up. He just looks at me. I then gently put him back into the water.

Now, the Lord tells me it's time to go. We hug, and I'm back home again.

155

Abraham Lincoln

If I'm away from the Lord for any length of time I get a yearning in my heart to see him. Just to gaze upon his face is extraordinary. When the Lord created us, He put a longing in our hearts for the supernatural, but some go over to the other side. I asked the Lord if I could come to his kingdom, and He said, "Anytime," which is tonight.

Now, I find myself in heaven in front of a fancy old house. I say old because it has vines growing up the sides and the brick looks weathered and worn. Suddenly, the Lord is standing beside me. He says, "Hi, how you doing, my son?"

"I'm fine Lord and yourself?"

"I'm fine too, my son." He motions with his hand, "Shall we go in?"

As the Lord knocks, I see someone through the window sitting on an old-fashioned chair in the living room getting up and coming to the front door. It opens and I recognize the person right away; it's Abraham Lincoln. "Come on in," he says warmly. "So, how are you two doing might I ask?"

I shake his hand, "We are fine."

Instead of marble floors like I have seen in other homes, his floors are wooden. The walls are adorned with paintings. He asks, "Would you both like a drop of tea?"

"Okay," the Lord and I say in almost perfect unison. He tells us to make ourselves at home, so the Lord and I move into the living room onto an old-fashioned couch, with ornate wooden sides to it.

Abe comes back with tea cups that have old pictures painted on them. I bet they would be very expensive if they were still on Earth! Abe turns to me and says, "I guess they would be at that." *He even heard my thoughts!* He sits next to the Lord with his legs crossed. He really looks relaxed.

I have to ask him, "So Abe, if you don't mind me calling you Abe."

"No, Richard, not at all. Go ahead. What were you going to ask?'"

"What was it like getting shot?" The Lord just looks at me.

"At first I heard a gunshot, then I felt a stinging sensation and felt kind of woozy. I don't really remember what came after that until my soul left my body. I looked at my body lying there on the bed and there were two angels waiting to escort me outside and up through the clouds, and here I am."

Abe looks to be in his early twenties. He doesn't have his famous beard, but you can tell it is Abraham Lincoln.

I ask Abe what's upstairs. He answers, "Oh nothing really, just bedrooms with beds, clothes etc."

"So, you like the old-fashioned way of putting clothes on?"

"Yes, other times I just think of things and they appear on me. It just depends on the mood I'm in." We both laugh. The Lord gets up and says, "Thank you for the tea, Abraham, it was delicious."

"Oh, you're quite welcome. Do you want some of my freshly baked cookies for the road?"

"No, I'm good," I reply. We all hug each other good-bye then shut the door behind us.

"Well my son, did you enjoy that?"

"Wow, that was fantastic Lord," I say excitedly. "I loved every minute of it.

The Lord says, "Okay, my son, your time is up. You have to be going now. I'll see you later." So, we hug and now I'm back home.

Butterflies Again

"Come on, I'm waiting" the Lord speaks into my heart. Earlier in the day I asked him if I could just come for a visit. His reply was, "You can come anytime." Tomorrow I have to be at work. I'd rather be in heaven, I hear people say all the time. But, when their physical bodies get sick most people go to the doctors first rather than the Lord. *Do you know anybody like that?*

The Lord playfully says, "I'm still waiting, my son!" Some people have said it's not good to keep the Lord waiting, but they don't have the relationship I have with him. I answer, "Yeah, yeah, I'm coming." So, now I'm walking up to the front gates, just being one of the crowd, minding my own business, when all of a sudden the Lord appears, saying, "Well."

I reply, "Well what?"

"What took you so long to get here?"

All I can think to say is "Oh, just being me I guess."

He looks at me with love in his eyes then puts his hands on my shoulders. "My son, a lot of people went to church today that ordinarily don't go. This always happens on Easter Sunday year-after-year. They go to appease their conscience and live like they want to the rest of the year."

159

I'm holding my breath for what he's going to say next. "I am not going to waste my time on these people any longer. I have tried them, but they refuse to listen to me. So, from this time on, I will leave them alone. Just like the Israelites, when they left Egypt. Their sandals never wore out, I fed them and took care of them, but they still died in the wilderness never reaching the Promised Land."

"What do you think about that, my son?"

"Well Lord, I think that's a really good idea. You have tried them, but to no avail. So, just leave them alone and concentrate on the remnant."

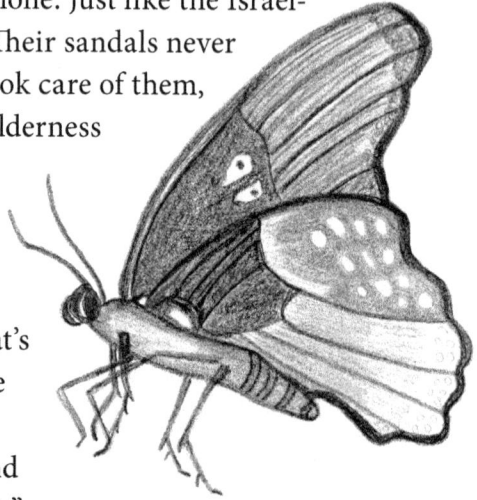

"That sounds good to me, now onto the brighter side of things."

We are just walking slowly up the main drag as the conversation continues. *By the way I have a big tall glass of chocolate milk. If I were on Earth I would definitely get a brain freeze!*

"My Father would like to know when you would like to visit him again. It's been awhile."

"Hmmm, I know, I miss him too, but I can't give you a definite time frame, okay?"

"Fine."

Just then a huge butterfly glides right by me. This is no ordinary butterfly, not like the ones I described in the other chapters.

I call to the Lord, "Did you see that?"

He laughs, "Yes I did, my son."

That butterfly was as big as a small child. I ask the Lord, "Why didn't you tell me about this before?"

160

"You weren't ready. I have many things in heaven you do not know of yet."

The butterfly lands next to me. It is yellow and the middle of its wings is a lighter yellow.

I reached out to touch one of its wings. It is kind of soft and rough at the same time. The Lord asks if I want to take a spin.

"You mean get on his back?"

"Exactly." He pulls me over to the middle between the two sets of wings.

Just then I notice some reins like you see on a horse, but these are much thinner.

I gently lift my leg and straddle it over the middle to the other side, then slide myself upright, grabbing the reins. This butterfly has silk-like hairs covering its middle. I yelled to the Lord, "Now what?"

"Just say, 'Let's go.'" The second I grabbed a hold of the reins, whoosh, we lifted off just like that. I can't believe I am actually riding a giant butterfly! *Those of you who are saying, "Yeah right! There's no such thing." Just wait until you get here.*

The take-off isn't a jolt; it is a gradual ascent. The butterfly is so graceful I don't even feel us going higher, when to my surprise, we are already at the tree tops. I can hear the whoosh of wind as the butterfly flaps its wings. I call turn to the left and immediately we turn. Then, we turn right. Next, we start gliding down to where the Lord is standing. I scoot off, "Wow Lord, I've never had so much fun!"

"You think? Now it is time for you to go, my son. The next time you're here you can ask to ride on a different colored one. So, we hug and now I'm back home again.

Throne Room of the Father

The Lord asks, "Would you like to meet?" Of course I would. Who wouldn't like a chance to go to heaven! Instantly I'm there. After going so many times, He almost always meets me at a certain place for a reason, and this time is no different.

We meet on the main street of heaven, which is always different colors of gold. This time the Lord asks, "Would you like to go see the Father?"

I replied, "Sure." So, we find ourselves outside a huge building with two columns on the outside that look like marble. There are two white doors with gold handles in the middle.

There are about forty long steps leading to the doors. The Lord and I get to the first set of steps, and I say to Him, "Watch this," and bam, I'm at the top step just like that.

The Lord claps his approval saying, "Very good, my son. You're getting there." As I'm standing there I hear praise coming from inside that sounds like a chorus of voices.

In a spit second, the Lord is standing beside me, motioning towards the door saying, "Shall we?"

I stop and say, "Lord, wait just a moment. I need a second." *It's not every day you meet the Lord's Father.* I take four deep breaths before saying, "Okay, let's go." Opening the door my eyes take a second to get used to the brightness.

Next, my eyes are met by an angel standing in front of me, dressed in a shimmering white robe. He has long shoulder-length blond hair, brown eyes, and sandals on his feet. We are in a front hallway and have to turn to the left after we enter.

The angel smiles and motions me to the left. My ears are met with loud praises as we approach a big room at the end of this hallway. This hallway is not narrow, by any means. As we get closer to the room, all of a sudden my knees start to feel kind of weak. I grab onto the Lord's arm as we continue walking down the hallway.

We enter the room and all I can see are angels everywhere, row upon row at least fifty deep. My eyes look over to the center of the room where I see a huge golden ornate throne-like chair. This is where the Father is sitting. I see a rainbow over the throne. The angels are shouting Glory, Glory, Glory. I noticed that all eyes are focused on me as I stand there in awe.

What I see next, near the throne, may alarm you, but the Bible talks about this. There are two Cherubim angels. They have four wings, each oval-shaped, and four eyes. They are about ten feet tall and are standing on each side of the throne. Their eyes remind me of the dragonfly eyes big with colors and are looking straight ahead.

I don't know what they are saying, but I hope it is something good! I try looking right at the Father, but I can't see all of him due to His glory. What I can see is part of his right leg to his toes, part of his right arm bent at the right chest area and part of his beard, just a bit more than my first time. He motions with his hand for me to come closer. It's kind of hard to see his hand because of all the mist, which is his glory. At this point the Lord is standing right behind me which is good, because I most probably would be on my back.

I move a bit closer to him. As I do, I hear in my mind, "Yes, my son, the angels are saying nice things about you." I stop about a foot away from the Father. At this point He puts out his hand and I grab onto it. It is really warm and big, I can fit two of my hands in his. He says to me in actual words with his mouth, "Do what I have put into your heart to do, regardless of what man says to you."

I let go of his hand, saying in my mind, "Lord may I speak?"

"Yes go ahead."

"I just want to say thank you for sending your son, Jesus, to die for me!" I turn to the Lord and give him a big hug.

"The Father says you're quite welcome, my son. Now, you have to be going." I wave good-bye to the Father, then hug the Lord. Now I'm back.

Spare Parts

I come floating towards the Lord near the singing fountain. I just float down as He says, "Good stuff, my son. I have been awaiting your arrival." Then He laughs and puts his arm around me. "It's good to see you, would you like to see something?" I wonder what He has up his sleeve.

In a split second, we both are standing outside a building with two wooden doors that are oval shaped at the top with two gold handles. Pushing them open, the first things I see are angels, about ten in all, putting body parts on tables. Legs, arms, toes, noses, eyeballs, anything that you could think of is there.

It's not like a horror show on TV. The bodies are not mutilated or anything like that. It's more like a hospital setting, very sterile and clean. The Lord says, "These parts you see are waiting for people to claim them, whatever they are in need of. I put the person's name below. This table is for the bigger parts like arms and legs.

The table is a white wood, and stands about five feet high. I notice that one of the tables has name plates in front of the parts. I also observe that some of the angels are taking them away. So, I turn to the Lord and ask where they were taking the spare parts. He answered, "People are requesting them."

I also noticed some angels taking the name plates off some of the limbs! I question the Lord about this and He says, "People of little faith talk people out of receiving their new limbs. You must believe with your whole being every part of my word. I'll give you an example; I spoke the world into existence, I had to believe with my whole being."

"Just like when I called Lazarus from the dead. I didn't look at the physical limitations; I saw beyond. I believed with my whole being that when I spoke, Lazarus' spirit and soul would return to his body. I had no doubt; you must be the same way."

As we get to the front door, I turn to the Lord, asking, "Where to Lord?" Just then I have a chocolate ice cream cone with chocolate syrup on it. *Oh, by the way; I have mentioned this before, but the ice cream here in heaven does not melt and always stays cold.* Before the Lord can answer, I suggested we go swimming in the river that flows from His throne.

He answers by saying, "I thought you would never ask!" Suddenly I'm in red and black swim trunks and the Lord is in light blue ones! They go down just above the knees, no Speedo for me. I see all the wounds the Roman solders inflicted on him, again not so pretty looking, but still beautiful to me.

Next, I find myself in a park setting. As we walk along, there is a river running right through the middle of the park. It looks to be about ten feet across. The water is crystal clear, flowing in a southern direction. "Are you ready, my son?"

"Yeah, I am ready when you are. On three, okay?" I say, raising my voice a little because I'm so excited! One, two, three! Bam! We both hit the water at the same time. The water is so refreshing. I can't touch the bottom it's so deep.

166

The Lord looks as though He is hardly moving at all. I know He's treading water. He calls to me, "Are you ready, my son?" I know what he's talking about. "Okay, let's go!" The Lord and I are neck and neck. We swim about a mile or so. When we stop the Lord says, "My son, your time is up." We hug in the water, and now I'm back.

Singing Fountain Again

Okay, I'll admit it. I have trouble pulling myself away from the TV. My flesh wants it and it is a war, but praise the Lord, my spirit man wins out. Now, I'm in heaven at the pearly gates. The Lord meets me and says, "Good to see you, my son, I see you found your way." We both laugh.

"Well, my son," He puts his arm around me, "don't worry, everything will be okay at work, you'll see." I don't even have to say what I am thinking. As I watch people walk by, I noticed a man riding a unicycle, *you know, like the ones you see in the circus. It strikes me as kind of funny, that's all.* I watch the unicycle go by, then I start to run after it, yelling "Hey, wait!"

When he stops, I ask if he could let me try it, he says, "Sure."

As I lower the seat to sit on it, he helps me up, pushes me forward, and I'm off. Wow! I'm actually riding a unicycle and I don't even fall once. When I get back to where the Lord is, He asks me, "Where do you want to go, my son?"

I say the fountain in the center of heaven. Bam! We are there in an instant.

I will refresh your memory this fountain has three tiers, stands about ten feet high, and is made out of white marble. The

168

top tier is much smaller than the other two but still looks big. As the water cascades down the sides, one can hear a sound like a singing choir, and the other two sides are making their own music, all in perfect harmony with each other. The bottom tier is so big one could go swimming in it and still have plenty of room.

The Lord says, "People come from all over heaven just to sit and listen to the harmony of sounds." Every once in a while the sounds change. I'm feeling a bit mischievous and start splashing the Lord. I get him good, and you know what He does? He starts splashing me back! When we finish, we are both completely soaked.

When you get wet in heaven it never lasts very long. I take a sip of water, umm, really good and refreshing, but the water isn't like water here on Earth. It flows through your fingers differently.

I say to the Lord, "I wish I wasn't here part-time. I know I have asked you plenty of times."

He puts his arm around me, saying, "Tell my people that I'm coming soon, very soon; in their lifetime. I'm getting the remnant ready for my return." Then He says, "It's time to go now, my son."

"Lord, I feel like I just got here! Come on, just another couple of minutes, please?"

"Okay."

"Thank you," I say with a sigh of relief.

Now, I'm at the gates again, just watching people come and go. *Remember, one has just to think of going somewhere and bam, you're there. I feel that I really haven't accomplished much, but I'm here in heaven and that's all that matters.* Here comes the Lord telling me it's time; now I'm back.

David's House

I was so tired last night that I asked the Lord if I could postpone my visit until today. My wife is going to the church for a women's meeting, so I will be alone. This is the perfect time to spend with the Lord.

Now, I'm in heaven, walking down the main drag, where I think the Lord might be. He likes to shake hands with a lot of people. Ah, just as I thought; He's shaking hands. I walk up and shake His hand also.

He says, "Glad to meet you, what's your name?" I know He is just kidding. Then He says, "Come on."

"Where to?"

"To King David's house!"

"Oh yes, sure." We walk past the pearly gates, and go about two miles, which takes us about a minute, and soon arrive at a two-story brick house with a lot of rose bushes in front; they are so brilliant in color.

The Lord mentions that David likes roses a lot. He sends me to knock on the front door. It's made of very expensive wood; *nothing is cheap in heaven.* It has solid gold door knockers and door handles, but no place for a deadbolt. *No one is going to steal from your home in heaven!* Then the big door opens.

King David is standing there. "Welcome, I've been expecting you! The Lord told me you were coming over today, so I made some of your favorite cookies and a tall glass of cold milk." I'm sure my mouth fell to the ground. I just never thought of David the mighty warrior as being gentle, humble, and making cookies!

He says, "Come on in," waving his hand and gesturing. We step onto big marble floors with a touch of gold running through them and then turn to the right into his living room. I sit down on one of the big leather couches, and the Lord sits next to me. David hands me a plateful of cookies, chocolate chip. Yum, so good. Just the way I like them, a little crunchy.

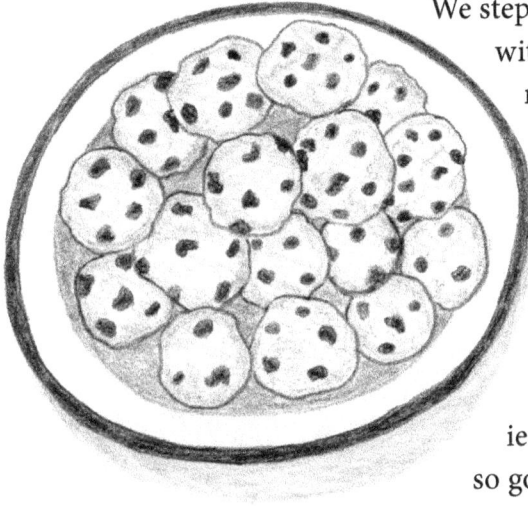

Next, he puts the glass of milk on the glass coffee table. It's crystal with four round pillars of pure gold holding it up! I put the tip of my finger on the glass, making it sing. I ask David where his crown is. He says, "Oh it's upstairs in my room. I just didn't feel like wearing it."

I ask, "So, what do you do all day?"

He smiles, "Well, I sometimes take long walks in one of the many parks, go on balloon rides, or talk to various people. You know, that kind of stuff."

It was mostly the things I do when I go to heaven. "I see you're wearing street clothes. That's cool." He laughs, "Yeah I feel more comfortable in them."

"Other than wearing a robe, have you ever worn clothes from the 1800s?"

His eyes light up, "Oh yes, some of them are very stylish, just wait a moment." He gets up and disappears around the corner. When he comes back he is carrying a long green overcoat.

I exclaim, "Wow!" as I touch one of the sleeves. It's made of silk. I ask if I can try it on. "Sure," he says. It fits me just fine except the sleeves are a bit short.

I hand it back to him and the Lord just laughs. I gulp down the rest of my milk just in time for the Lord to say "Well, my son, it's time for you to leave."

I reply, "Nah, really? You must be thinking of someone else!"

"No," was his reply. I hug David and the Lord in a group hug then say good-bye to both of them.

Now, I'm transported back to Earth.

Fishing

I'm waiting," I hear the Lord say softly in my heart. Just that fast I'm in glory. Nothing even comes close to the Lord's glory. There are no words to describe it. I find myself in a forest setting, which is nothing new. The Lord meets me by the edge where the bushes start to get thick. He says, "Nice for you to come along, my son.

I just laugh, "Yeah."

"Lord, have I been in this forest before?"

"No my son, not this particular one."

We were going someplace, I just didn't know where. The Lord says, "Just follow me. You can only get there on foot. It's one of my favorite places."

So, we march on. *In your new body nothing bothers you; you don't sweat or get tired.*

Wow! I'm glad there's no mosquitoes or they'd be eating me alive, that's if I did the same thing on Earth. The brush is starting to thin out a bit, the Lord is still leading the way. We come to a clearing with a beautiful lake with trees all around. What a beautiful sight. The Lord asks if I would like to go fishing. I jumped at the chance, and found myself jumping up and down. Fishing with the Lord, who wouldn't want to do that!

"Just one thing," I say looking around, "I don't see a boat!"

The Lord replies, "We don't need one." *Just imagine the look on my face when He said that. I thought we would just stay on the shore.* The fishing rods showed up instantly. In his hand were two white ones with hooks. He says, "Follow me and do what I do."

"Sure, lead the way." There is a slight sandbar at the edge of the water. The Lord puts one foot slowly on top of the water, so I can see what He is doing. He does the same with his other foot and continues on.

"Okay, I'm going to do the same." I put my foot near the sandbar and it stays on top of the water. Then I put my other foot on top of the water. I don't sink, just like the time before at the duck pond.

He says, "Come on, let's go," and starts walking normally across the water. After a few moments, we are both in the middle of the lake. He stops and says, "Okay, let's put our hooks in!"

I exclaim, "What!? No bait!?" It reminds me of when the Lord told the disciples to put down their nets on the opposite side of the boat. They obeyed, even though they had been fishing all night without catching anything.

I put down my hook and right away I get a bite. It looks like a bass; maybe a five pounder. I'm beside myself. I'm standing in the middle of a lake beside the Lord of Glory and fishing without any bait on my hook. *Can you even picture that?* I ask the

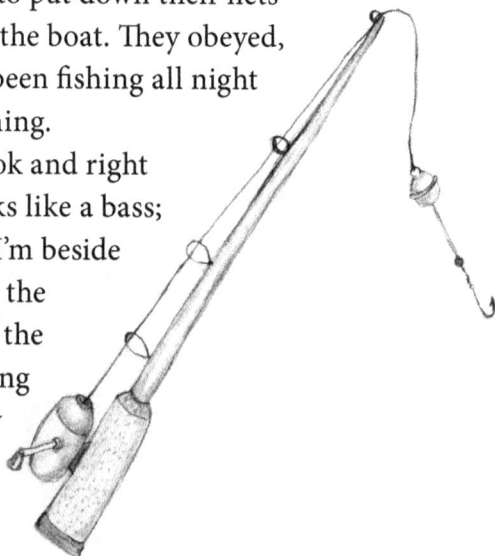

174

Lord, "What do you want me to do with the fish?" He tells me to throw it back.

After a while He turns to me. "My son, it's time for you to go."

I reply, "You must be thinking of someone else, Lord?"

He looks me in the eyes, saying in an almost whispering tone, "My son, it's time for you to go."

We hug and now I'm back.

A Spot of Tea

I got home early today from work, and I plan to see the Lord. He says to me, "You can come here now," and Bam, I'm in heaven. My spirit man is transported just that fast. The Lord meets me in my tree house on the couch. I never know for sure where I am going to meet the Lord. All that pops into my head is to say, "What's going on, Lord?"

He laughs, "Good to see you too, my son."

The Lord has a cup of coffee in his hand, but it smells like flowers not coffee. *You know, the flowers they make tea with.*

"Would you like some tea, my son?"

"Yes," is my reply and instantly a cup of tea appears in my hand. The mug is made up of expensive crystal, but the funny thing is that my tea is very hot while the outside of the mug is cold, like it was in the fridge overnight.

"How is that, Lord?"

"How is what, my son?"

"That the outside is cold while the inside is piping hot?"

He laughs. "Well my son, it's just the opposite of how things are on Earth. Remember the flowers that tasted like they looked?"

"Yeah," I said, wondering where he's going with this.

"I use the simple things to confuse the wise, not just on Earth. There are many things in heaven that confuse man's mind. Remember, my ways are above man's ways, even more so in heaven."

"I'll give you one more example. Remember the faucets on your bathtub. There are no pipes running to them, but water still flows out! Plus, there are no hot water heaters in heaven. *Many people reading this are wondering how could these things be?*"

I finished the last drop of tea. As I glanced at the bottom of my cup, it is instantly filled again. My mind went to where the Lord had told me only if I wanted it to fill again it would.

On my coffee table sits a dish of chocolate cookies with marshmallows inside. I take one and dip it into my tea. The Lord takes one too.

Just as I'm sinking into the couch again, the Lord says, "Well, my son, I have some pressing work to do, so if you don't mind, I'll be getting back."

"Yeah, Lord, I'll let you go. So long for now."

We hug and now I'm back.

Sunflowers

I'm in my room all alone with just my table lamp beside me. It's not that bright so as not to distract me. The Lord says, "Okay, I'm waiting for you to arrive." Now, I'm in heaven. *I love my eternal home. Can you imagine that throughout eternity I'll be with the Lord, the one who loves me no matter what?* The Lord meets me in a big field of sunflowers.

These aren't just your ordinary run of the mill sunflowers, they are gigantic. The petals and the inner core that holds the seeds are as big as dinner plates. The stems are about eight to ten feet tall. I have written about flowers in fields before, but these by far are the best. These aren't planted in nice little rows, they are all scattered around.

On Earth sunflowers mostly have yellow petals and are dark brown where the seeds are. These flowers are 34 different colors. The Lord is standing beside me, enjoying the flowers also. I ask him, "Why are these sunflowers all different colors?"

"Well, my son, that's how heaven is. Earth was created in the likeness of heaven, but it's different."

As I start walking, I push some of them aside. Now I'm looking over them, because I'm standing on a small hill. There must be over a billion, as far as I can see there are sunflowers.

It is amazing to have flowers that are taller than you are. I bend one over to smell it, and it smells like a rose! I'm not kidding. I'm trying to wrap my head around it all.

So, naturally I ask the Lord, "Why do they smell like roses?"

He laughs, "Heaven is different from Earth, remember?"

"Yeah, I remember."

"My son, a lot of Earth rules don't apply here. You should know that by now."

"Yeah, Lord, but some things still surprise me."

He laughs again. I have a tall glass of milk, just because. I crouch down, looking at all the stems here and there; it's different from looking from above them. I decide to take a short walk and explore. That's why I'm not walking in a straight line. Suddenly, a butterfly with blue wings lands on my hand. It isn't nearly as big as the ones we rode. I look back, but I don't see the Lord anywhere! I call out, "Lord, are you there?" No answer. I'm not afraid or anything like that. Perhaps he's playing with me. I yell, "Ready or not, here I come."

I start retracing my steps, all the time

179

hollering, "Okay, I'm going to find you. Here I come!" After about ten minutes, I'm back to where I started from and still there's no trace of the Lord. It must be close to the time for me to go home. I have spent a lot of time here, which is good. As I make a turn, all of a sudden I feel arms around my waist!

"I got you! Ha, ha, ha!"

I knew it was the Lord, we both start laughing. Then He says, "Okay, it's really time for you to go home now. I mean your other home."

"Okay." We hug; now I'm back.

Nightlife

ord, I really need to see you tonight," I just finished saying. Turning around in my chair, I notice the Lord is sitting on the edge of my bed. "Lord," I exclaim, "how long have you been sitting there?"

"I just arrived, my son." He gets up to shake my hand. "It's good to see you."

"I love your sandals. The blue stones suit you."

He says, "They are blue sapphires."

I take a second look at the Lord, and ask, "Lord, are you all right? You seem kind of quiet."

"I'm just mellow, that's all. Where would you like to go?"

"Well," I say, rubbing my chin in thought, "Lord, take me somewhere I've never been before." *You know, with a statement like that, we could end up literally anywhere.*

It only takes him a second to answer, "Okay, hold my hand." I do, and now we are both flying through the air. Up, up we go. Suddenly, we stop in mid-air and start going north. It reminds me of flying in an airplane at low altitude, looking at all the lights. Now, I find myself going down, slowing in speed. We touch down, and I can't help but think this place looks familiar.

We're in Times Square, New York City with the big jumbotron. I look around, "Lord, look at all these people. Where are they going?"

He answers, "My son, it's what they call fun! But actually, it's not. You have restaurants that serve liquor, nearby you have strip clubs, and you have 'bookie clubs' where people pay to bet on anything."

"Lord, can they see us?"

"No, not unless you want them to."

We are in the middle of the street, with people milling all around and walking right though us, which is kind of fun.

"Lord, are there any 'ladies of the night' here," I ask, trying to put it nicely. He smiles at me, saying, "Of course, but not right here, as this is more a tourist place. Come with me."

I take him by the hand again, and instantly we seem to be about five blocks away from where we were just standing. This place is not a dumpy neighborhood, it's upper middle class. He says, "Look over there," as He points to two women standing off to one side, just hanging out. Both of them have casual clothes on, but their skirts reveal almost everything, leaving little for the imagination. They're also wearing short matching sweater tops and high heels. I bet they are wearing wigs too, but I can't tell for sure since it is dark.

The Lord says to me, "Come on, let's go." He takes me by my hand. *At this point you would want them to see you. I just had to think that and I became visible.* We don't have any robes on or anything like that, just casual street clothes. As we come closer, one of them says, "Hi honey, how you all doing?" I let them know we are fine. The second girl looks right at me and says, "Are you both up for a little excitement?"

I say, "We're just enjoying the scenery."

I guess the girls took my statement the wrong way. I think she thinks I am complimenting their bodies, because they start walking closer to us. Then the Lord starts to talk to them. *I thought He would never start.* He asks the shortest one her name. She replies, "Charlotte."

"Oh, that's a nice name." He turns to the other girl and asks her the same question. She reveals her name is Cynthia. The Lord just looks at her. He turns back to Charlotte and asks her how long she has been on the streets.

"Oh, about five years."

The Lord just says, "Hmmm." Then He starts literally telling her life story from when she was about five years old to the present. She was abused when younger, got into drugs, then met a pimp.

At this point Charlotte has tears in her eyes. She asks, "Who are you? The Lord then rolls up his sleeves, exposing the nail scars above his wrists. By this time she is sobbing uncontrollably! She is in shock and disbelief, for she knows who is standing in front of her.

She kneels in front of Him saying, "Lord, forgive me of my many sins! I will follow you the rest of my life." The Lord puts His hand on one of her shoulders saying, "I will forgive you, now I call you my daughter."

At this she starts crying again, and then she stands up and gives him a big hug, wiping her tears away with her hand as her mascara streaks down her cheeks.

At this point, Cynthia is trying to make sense of all this. I guess she needs more time to think about things. The Lord takes two steps toward her and puts his hand against one of her cheeks, as He lovingly looks into her eyes.

Now, we are both back in my bedroom. The first thing I say is, "Wow! That was way cool, Lord."

He replies, "Yes, that was very nice indeed, now I have to be going." We hug; then He is gone.

I Know

I know you have made many choices in life,
some good, some bad.
I have been watching over your life
for many years now.
The reason being,
I wish you to be with me
in paradise for eternity.

I created you before this world began,
yes even before the dinosaurs.
Make no mistake; this is me,
the one who sits on high and sees low.
It's not often I speak through my servants,
like a nursery rhyme, but in your case,
I'll make an exception.

Do you know I would love to call you my own,
for you I died on the cross alone.
If you were the only person alive,
I would have done it all for you.
I know you have gone through
many trials in your life,

when the chips were down,
I had mercy on your life.
I'm calling you to myself,
we both know your time is coming to a close.
So why not give me your whole self,
before your time finally runs out.

I know your comings and your goings,
even down to the very hairs on your head.
If you think this world has everything you need,
you are sadly mistaken.
It has nothing over me.

I have a different plan for your life,
but I still love you just the same.
I cry for all the souls I have created.
I pray it's not in vain.
I will still love them, and you,
throughout eternity.

About the Author

RICHARD S. SMITH lives in Florida with his wife Josephine, and his cat. He likes a good cup of coffee sitting on his front porch after a summer's rain or even during one. He has a passion for old cars, but he only has one. Richard went to college to finish his studies as a jeweler. When he's not looking at diamonds and gold to buy on line he enjoys a good game of chess. In his spare time he enjoys a brisk bike ride to stay in shape.

For relaxation Richard enjoys playing the piano, at which he is self-taught. Taking full advantage of living in Florida he also enjoys spending time with his wife while fishing at the nearby waterfront.

Since college Richard has worked at various occupations. But none have been more fulfilling than his current occupation; writing about visiting heaven. In his book, *Glimpses of Heaven*, Richard shares his love and passion which is richly enveloped in his experiences about visiting heaven.

I'd love to read what you thought of this book. Please leave your honest review at http://a.co/d91ur3Y.

Stay connected with
Richard S. Smith

Be among the first to
be notified about his
upcoming books

FOLLOW ME

Facebook:
Richardsmithglimpsesofheaven

Twitter:
Snowwyite

Instagram:
glimpsesofheaven01

www.ingramcontent.com/pod-product-compliance
Lightning Source LLC
LaVergne TN
LVHW041316080426
835513LV00008B/490